W9-DFS-441

ADVENTURE
IN SPIRITUAL DIRECTION:
A PROPHETIC PATTERN

Adventure in Spiritual Direction: A Prophetic Pattern

Roman Ginn, o.s.c.o.

LIVING FLAME PRESS

BOX 74 LOCUST VALLEY, N.Y. 11560

253.5
Gi A

The New American Bible is used in quotations:

Nihil Obstat: Rev. George A. Denzer, D.D., S.T.D.
Censor Librorum
May 21, 1979

Imprimatur: Most Reverend John R. McGann, D.D.
Bishop of Rockville Centre
June 1, 1979

Cover: Robert Manning

Published by Living Flame Press / Locust Valley / New York 11560

Copyright © 1979: Roman Ginn o.c.s.o.

ISBN 0-914544-27-6

All rights reserved. This book or parts thereof must not be reproduced in any form without the permission of the publisher.

Printed in the United States of America.

Table of Contents

Introduction

The fourth book of the Pentateuch is called Numbers because some of its chapters are full of numbers, especially census numbers. Consequently some of its pages are as dry as the Sinai Desert, the scene for much of its action. But just as this desert has its oases, so Numbers contains some of the most colorful narratives in the Old Testament, among which is the delightful and even humorous story of Balaam and Balak. The main purpose of this episode, which took place in the thirteenth century B.C. in the land of Moab, is to demonstrate God's power over all occult forces of magic and divination. But this doesn't exhaust its meaning, for this narration is also a rich source of doctrine on an important spiritual problem of our day: spiritual direction.

Balaam is only coming into his own today, for this enigmatic figure has suffered for centuries from a bad press. In the story in Numbers, he is clearly a good man and a friend of Israel but other texts in the Old Testament present him as a bad man who advised the Midianite women to lead the Israelites into sin *(Numbers 31:16),* and so deserved to be put to death as Israel's enemy *(Numbers 31:8).* Subsequent Jewish tradition, the New Testament *(2 Peter 2:15f; Jude v. II; Revelation 2:14),* and most Patristic tradition preserved this hostile view of Balaam. Fortunately, however, Christian art softened this opinion and found room for him, his humble burro and his star on sarcophagi, church doors and ceilings, and in many paintings.

The reason for the confusion about this fascinating prophet has only recently been discovered by biblical scholars. They have shown that in pre-Israelite oral tradition, he is presented as a powerful, honest and faithful servant of God. This more favorable view of Balaam continued for some seven centuries throughout the transmission of the story in written form by the Israelite historians. It was only when he fell into the hands of a later group of theologians who gave the Pentateuch its final form — the Sacerdotal school — that the prophet became a scoundrel and Israel's archenemy. This sudden change seems to have been due to their exegetical interpretation of the story rather than to any historical tradition. But whatever the reasons, Balaam emerged as a bad man and passed into history as such. And now that his good name has finally been restored, the true nature of his relationship to the king of Moab becomes clear. Balaam was not only a soothsayer, prophet, diviner and visionary, but a counsellor and spiritual director as well.

The importance of the counsellor's office in the Ancient Near East can be seen in a text by Isaiah which names him among the key dignitaries of Israelite society *(Isaiah 3:2f)*. Jeremiah 18:18 and Ezekiel 7:26 place the counsellor on the same level as the priest and prophet. The Old Testament is full of references to him because society's life and salvation depended on his decisions *(e.g. 2 Samuel 16:23; 1 Kings 1:11f)*. A text from Micah states that Balaam's counsel prevailed over King Balak's plan to harm Israel *(Micah 6:5)*, and the prophet's final remark to the king is a word of counsel on Moab's future *(Numbers 24:14)*. Counsel was particularly necessary for political matters, but by no means restricted to them. The entire life of the nation and of the individual rested on sound counsel as Israel's wisdom literature clearly illustrates.

Modern biblical scholarship has uncovered a great deal of information on Balaam and the conditions in which he lived. It has shown, for example, that the figures of Balaam and Balak existed separately in tradition and were joined only later. It can now explain many of the small inconsistencies in the story. It has also stressed that throughout the centuries there was a constant effort in every period of its tradition to keep the story living and adapted to the needs of the time. The reflections that follow have the same intention in presenting Balaam as a great spiritual counsellor from the second millennium.

Spiritual direction at that time and outside Israel could hardly be expected to be the relatively simple, clear-cut function it is today. It was contaminated with magic and divination. If a modern spiritual director would notice a broken stick lying in the grass as he walked to his office, he would normally not interpret it as an omen or portent indicating that the first subject he interviewed was about to crack up under the strain of his sufferings. But in Balaam's day, this was good divination practice. If a counsellor was also a diviner, he had thousands of natural phenomena, from stars to animal entrails, which he could investigate to help him direct his spiritual client. We must not be surprised then when Balaam takes a bag of omens along to assist him in his directional work at the court of Moab. He may have had a cup in which he could observe the movement or configurations of drops of oil upon water, or some sticks to throw into the air so that their position on landing could be observed. We shouldn't be surprised either if he begins his four great oracles by the observation and interpretation of natural phenomena: a dust storm for the first, a rain storm for the second, running water for the third and a star for the final one. But in spite of the differences, Balaam and the modern spiritual director are essentially men of God trying to help others develop spiritually. They are both spiritual directors.

But if Balaam and Balak were separated in the earliest tradition, today their names are as inseparably linked as those of Barnum and Bailey. Accordingly we will treat the directional relationship between them from the point of view of Balaam, the director, and Balak, the subject receiving the direction. What is said about the director's part, however, is by no means without value for those who are not professional directors. For spiritual direction includes everything from a friendly passing counsel by one Christian to another in spiritual need, up to the professional director's habitual full dedication to someone seeking spiritual formation. Just as a knowledge of first aid is useful for non-physicians, so an elementary acquaintance with the principles of spiritual direction is useful for everyone seriously interested in the spiritual life. The Good Samaritan wasn't a doctor, but he gave first aid to the wounded man on the road and took care of him until he could hand him over to a professional. Every Christian, especially the Christian parent, will meet those in spiritual need whom he can help in an analogous way.

By following Balaam and Balak in their directional relationship, we can reflect on this wonderful mystery of man's cooperation with God in the sanctification of other men *(1 Corinthians 3:9)*, and observe it in action. The final step will be to put it into practice ourselves: "Each should please his neighbor so as to do him good by building up his spirit" *(Romans 15:2)*.

1

Balak Seeks Spiritual Help

Then the Israelites moved on and encamped in the plains of Moab on the other side
of the Jericho stretch of the Jordan. Now Balak,
son of Zippor, saw all that Israel did to the
Amorites. Indeed, Moab feared the Israelites
greatly because of their numbers, and detested
them. So Moab said to the elders of Midian,
"Soon this horde will devour all the country
around us as an ox devours the grass of the
field." And Balak, Zippor's son who was king of
Moab at that time, sent messengers to Balaam,
son of Beor, at Pethor on the Euphrates, in the
land of the Amawites, summoning him with
these words, "A people has come here from
Egypt who now cover the face of the earth and
are settling down opposite us! Please come and
curse this people for us; they are stronger than
we are. We may then be able to defeat them and
drive them out of the country. For I know that
whoever you bless is blessed and whoever you
curse is cursed." Then the elders of Moab and of

Midian left with the divination fee in hand and went to Balaam. When they had given him Balak's message, he said to them in reply, "Stay here overnight, and I will give you whatever answer the Lord gives me." So the princes of Moab lodged with Balaam.

Numbers 22:1-8

The little kingdom of Moab in the thirteenth century B.C. was highly organized with good agricultural and pastoral pursuits, splendid buildings, distinctive pottery, and strong fortifications. King Balak then had every reason to be happy, but he wasn't; for suddenly something new came into his life. Reports came in about a strong and numerous people who had fled from Egypt, crossed the Sinai Desert and were defeating nation after nation in their march toward Canaan. At present, they were camped at his frontier, and he was worried. Israel was a problem for Balak just as the great changes in the modern world present a problem to the Christian. But changes also represent new opportunities and during times of great change, great men frequently appear in the midst of the people of God to create new institutions, theologies and spiritualities. Men like Paul, Augustine and Bernard of Clairvaux are capable of transforming such novelties into new pathways to God and new ways of living the ancient faith. But like King Balak, many Christians don't feel capable of rising to the challenge alone, and are looking for some fellow Christian from whom they can receive guidance and support. Like Balak, they need spiritual direction.

Balak didn't realize that Israel's appearance meant that God was drawing near to him in a new way. He felt no need for a new road to God. He had grown up with certain religious practices and beliefs well assimilated into his existence and resented the questioning Israel brought into his life. The modern Christian has received his faith incarnated in certain intellectual, affective and sociological forms, and will naturally suffer when he sees these questioned and often discarded as inoperative. And although he knows that his faith transcends any form of expression and is capable of becoming incarnate in new forms that express it better in the new historical situation, he still feels alone and abandoned. His orientation points and supports have disappeared and he is looking for security. While Balak sent for a counsellor to curse the new things in his life, the modern Christian wants one to help him meet and accept them and come closer to God through them.

It might be objected that Balak isn't capable of receiving spiritual direction, for this demands an interior desire to give oneself to God even at the cost of self-sacrifice; while all the king of Moab was interested in was getting rid of his enemy. But to interpret the story in this way would be to impose our modern separation of the sacred and profane dimensions of reality onto the Ancient Near Eastern world. If Israel was winning and Moab losing, this was a clear indication to Balak that something was also spiritually wrong. His god

14

Chemosh must be mad about something again and the king wanted to find out what he had done wrong and what he would have to do to appease the god's anger. Thus there was a minimal spirit of conversion in his heart and some willingness to be corrected and directed. He wasn't seeking spiritual experience for itself, like some people today, but intended to give himself to Chemosh, whom he regarded as the true god. This is all that could be expected from a second millennium polytheist.

Balak's faith in Chemosh was like the dead stump of a tree: lifeless and unable to generate new bark as the old rots and falls off. But the Christian's faith is endowed with perennial youth and is capable of breaking the spiritual molds it is contained in and producing new ones, just as a living tree can shed old bark and grow new exterior coverings to protect and express it. This faith gives Christian spirituality its perpetual youth and enables it to constantly give birth to new saints, texts and practices which do not eliminate the old but are their homogenous substitution and prolongation. But everyone can't face this process with equal plasticity. Thus persons are needed who not only live with a deep personal experience of God themselves, but are capable of reflecting on that experience and communicating it to others. These individuals should guide the Christian from his first steps in the spiritual life to a full mystical experience. They should help him assimilate the truths of his faith that he has been carrying around in his mind like excess baggage and integrate them into his life in spite of all the changes going on around him. This is the task of the spiritual director.

Every change from one historical period to another means a disappearance of the cultural and religious scenery men have become accustomed to and this causes them to feel that the world has become insecure and threatening. It creates a desire to hold back change and return to the more commodious existence enjoyed before. This was Balak's reaction. But these novelties also offer man an opportunity to distance himself from the forms he has been living in and to return to the sources of his being from which the light that explains both it and his mission in the world arises. But no one is better qualified than a spiritual director to assist man on this journey to the sources.

Balak may have believed that the best way to meet the new world taking shape around him was by a restoration of the old. He didn't feel like creating anything new. Chemosh would probably be satisfied with a good polishing up of his statues, to bring out their original texture, and the people would probably be satisfied with a few much-needed rehearsals of the Baal-Peor sanctuary choir that would permit the native vigor of the ancient hymns to be heard again. This sort of advice was what he expected from his new spiritual director, that is, if he decided to put the care of his soul into his hands when he got to Moab and performed his curse. This restoration would nullify the danger Israel had introduced. Chemosh would be content and Balak could hold on to what he had with only an apparent change being made. Some Christians today have the same temptation. They prefer the security of a restoration to the risk of a new creation. But the security is only an apparent one and this easy imitation of former things will prove to be sterile in the long run. An accurate translation into another language can't be a material repetition of older translations, but must present the original in terms that correspond to it today. Christians can't be content with dusting off older forms and practices but must create those which translate the Gospel's values into our modern world. The spiritual director will help the individual to integrate his life into this new world and contribute to the creation of new forms of prayer, self-denial and fraternal love.

Israel's appearance at his doorstep immediately relativized many of the internal problems — domestic or political — that were troubling the royal mind. If one of his wives was not conducting herself properly or if his eldest son was drinking again, Israel's coming caused these things to shrink in size. The same phenomenon is being experienced in the modern Church. Internal problems that were burning issues a few years ago have lost their importance. They seemed monumental when contemplated from within, but lost much of their weight when the perspective shifted to the outside world. This healthy change of focus makes it possible to verify the faith before the world in a new way. But many find it hard to readjust alone and want a guide.

We who live in the post-Vatican II Church should feel real sympathy for this king of Moab. Like us, he saw immense changes coming into his world and his reaction to those which he saw as a personal threat was to curse them and so weaken them that his army could easily destroy them. He had to watch Israel absorb the values and standards he had grown up with "as an ox devours the grass of the field." Like many Christians today he needed a counsellor to help him find his place in the new order. His self-confidence, which Israel was shaking, had to be restored, and the vocation by which he should sanctify his life as well as the particular charism by which he should contribute to the world had to be rediscovered in their new context. He had heard of a certain Balaam, a Mesopotamian "baru," a soothsayer and diviner, a man with great clairvoyant gifts, a counsellor of unparalleled wisdom, a true spiritual guide. He would send for him at once. If he proved to be as great as his reputation, he would make him a father to the Moabite court just as Pharaoh made Joseph his father and "lord of all his household, and ruler over the whole land of Egypt" *(Genesis 45:8).*

Balak certainly knew how to select a spiritual director. He didn't send a delegation to ask Balaam directly to become his guide, but tested him first by presenting him with a particular problem. This gave him a chance to see if he was the right man. If the prophet manifested competence in handling this problem, Balak would make the relationship permanent, otherwise he would pack him off for home with no commitment. This is the way every Christian should go about finding a director. He should see first how he deals with a particular spiritual problem in his own life, and then make a decision. A director should never be chosen blindly or because of his reputation or some other purely human quality. What is medicine for some can be poison for others.

The text gives evidence that Balak was looking for a permanent spiritual counsellor and not a mere "baru" who cursed on order. For the king's thrice-repeated promise of a reward *(Numbers 22:17. 37; 24:11)* refers to honor and dignity rather than to a financial recompense. A position for Balaam such as Joseph received from Pharaoh would fit the situation better. Pharaoh was so delighted after Joseph explained his dream that he told him: "You shall be in charge of my palace, and all my people shall dart at your command. Only in respect to the throne shall I outrank you" *(Genesis 41:40).* In ancient society money didn't have the supreme importance it has today, when there are so many more things to buy. If Balaam only referred to money in his reply to Balak *(Numbers 22:18; 24:13),* it was a sign of his delicacy of feeling toward his host, whom he didn't want to embarrass by anticipating his intentions too much. This makes Balaam's fidelity to God all the more remarkable. He preferred obedience to the divine word to a high position in the Moabite court.

Balak gives us another solid lesson in choosing a director; he only sent for one. On this point

St. John of Avila, one of the Church's great spiritual directors, has this to say: "...although we should have peace with all, we should be satisfied with the counsel of one. For as in corporeal matters, many hands are more likely to confuse things than to put them in order, the same is true in spiritual matters, where you will seldom find two guides that entirely agree; unless they be well instructed by the Lord's Spirit, which is a Spirit of peace and union, and can keep their own opinions at a distance; for these are the cause of diversity and squabbles. But because this type is rarely found, it is good — without saying anything bad about others — to choose whomever God sends you, 'one among a thousand,' to whom in the Lord's name you should bend your ear with all obedience and security."

Ordinarily in every religious family some elementary spiritual direction is given by the parents. So Balak probably had already received a rudimentary spiritual formation at home. The early Christians certainly formed their children spiritually, as is clear from a case like Timothy's, whom Paul reminds of the faith he received as an inheritance: "I find myself thinking of your sincere faith — faith which first belonged to your grandmother Lois and to your mother Eunice..." *(2 Timothy 1:5)*. Paul also refers to his disciple's early acquaintance with sacred Scripture, another sign of his mother's direction *(2 Timothy 3:15ff)*. Both Paul and Balaam only needed to perfect and continue the directional work already begun.

20

It must be stressed that Balak freely sent for Balaam. The initiative was entirely the king's. He was so sure he wanted the Mesopotamian mystic that he sent a new delegation after the first had been turned down. He wasn't moved by a moral obligation but by a vital impulse of his being. He needed help and called for it. The Christian today knows by theological reflection that direction is a morally necessary means for spiritual growth; necessary to make up for his inability to follow the motions of the Spirit by himself. Humility demands that he recognize and accept this inability. But to seek spiritual direction only because one feels morally bound to do so means approaching it along the wrong road.

St. John of the Cross' solid advice about choosing a director applies to Balak's case. "It is very necessary that one who wishes to advance in recollection and perfection be aware into whose hands he is placing himself, for as the master, so the disciple, and as the father, so the son" *(Living Flame 3, 30)*. Yet the saint insists on the need for direction. "The soul that is alone, without a master and virtuous is like a lighted coal that is alone: it will get cooler rather than warmer" *(Words of Light #7)*. There can be no doubt that many Christians never develop spiritually because there is no one to help them. By creating man as a social being, God willed that we help each other in spiritual as well as material matters. Consequently the choice of a director is one of the most important decisions in a man's life. Balak did well to choose carefully.

When a director has been chosen, an implicit contract is made by which the subject agrees to manifest his conscience and allow himself to be guided, and the director compromises himself to earnestly try to lead him to God. A manifestation of conscience is an explanation of the interior motives, dispositions and feelings which are the sources of our exterior conduct. The director has the right to put questions discreetly in response to this manifestation. We see then why Balaam was slow in answering the king's call. He realized the seriousness of his office and wanted to consult the Lord before accepting such a task.

From the mere director-subject point of view and aside from qualifications that might be made because of other elements in the situation, a director never has the right to demand a manifestation of conscience. This would mean doing violence to conscience. If things ever reach this point, the subject should look elsewhere for a guide. Balaam never tried to cross-examine his royal subject. He accepted his reasons for calling him at face value and respected his liberty entirely.

If Balaam had been living under the New Covenant he would have been even more careful about accepting such a responsibility, for in the Church the choice of a director means entering upon a state of discipleship with Christ through the director. This means that the subject will try to conform his judgments and criteria to those of the director in order to pass through him into a better understanding of the Gospel. As St. Paul, the director should be a living image of Christ whom the subject can imitate by imitating him. "Imitate me as I imitate Christ" *(1 Corinthians 11:1).* The director is thus an evangelical counsellor who applies the demands and doctrine of the Gospel to the subject. But he will do so by counsel and not by command, since he has no authority to command.

Balaam knew that an incompetent director could do more harm than an incompetent physician, for the latter destroys men's bodies while the director ruins their souls. The director's capital sin is pointed out in the Gospel when Jesus refers to the blind leading the blind *(Matthew 15:14).* Domination, by which the subject's efforts at spiritual maturation — which direction is supposed to be furthering — are suffocated, is another sin in direction. Instead of helping him learn to make his own decisions, a domineering director violates the subject's autonomy by imposing his own ideas. Instead of seeing what Christ wants from the individual, the director only considers what he wants, thus substituting himself for Christ. Sometimes this even comes out in words: "Now, my child, this is what I want from you." Balaam was too aware that he was only the Lord's instrument to ever speak words like this.

The Old Testament gives an example of the results of bad counselling in King Rehoboam, who turned down the wise advice of the old men who had served his father and preferred the counsel of his playmates *(1 Kings 12:6ff)*. Disaster for the country followed. The playmates may have been called counsellors and may have exercised the function, just as one can be a physician and do everything but cure, but they lacked the qualifications. Balak knew that there were charlatans among counsellors as in all other professions. He took great pains to be sure he was putting his soul in the hands of a true man of God.

Just as natural parenthood brings the right and duty to educate children, so the Church has the obligation and right to form its children. After engendering divine life in them, it must guide them to spiritual maturity. When Jesus told his disciples, "Go, therefore, and make disciples of all the nations . . . teach them to carry out everything I have commanded you" *(Matthew 28:19f)*, he pointed to a relationship between these new disciples and their masters that corresponds to his relationship to his disciples while on earth, one that was personal and formative. St. Paul was careful to educate the new Christians he had converted, revisiting them, writing to them, spending long periods with them and giving personal direction whenever possible, as with Timothy, Mark and others. He didn't think that baptism and catechism were enough, but wanted to make "every man complete in Christ" *(Colossians 1:28)*. The faithful can and should look to the Church for a spiritual education, and one of the best means of obtaining this is through spiritual direction. Balaam didn't need to be told that no one can learn divination or any other art

24

without a teacher and he had learned that teaching men to live with God was the most difficult form of education to impart, for men simply don't like to follow the Spirit.

St. Augustine remarks that even though St. Paul received a heavenly vision *(Acts 9:3-7),* he was sent to a man to receive the sacraments. And that although an angel told the centurion Cornelius that his prayers had been accepted *(Acts 10:1-6),* he was sent to St. Peter for the sacraments and indoctrination. God could have done all this through an angel, but it would have appeared to be a depreciation of man and an indication that he didn't care to speak to men through other men, and that although man was God's temple, he didn't want to speak through that temple *(Christian Doctrine, Prologue 6, 7).* Balaam realized that God spoke through weak men like himself and would not have been surprised to learn that in the New Covenant he spoke through his Church.

Balak knew he was in trouble and sent for a counsellor. Many Christians today don't know what is wrong with them. They are like Moses who was unnecessarily wearing himself out judging the people all day until his father-in-law Jethro came along and said: "You are not acting wisely . . . Now listen to me . . ." *(Exodus 18:17ff).* Fortunately, "Moses followed the advice of his father-in-law and did all that he had suggested" *(v. 24).*

We don't know how many calls Balaam got for spiritual direction, but today many a director is almost unemployed, for direction is in a state of crisis. Many Christians don't like to hear the subject mentioned. While oriental gurus, fortune-tellers, astrologers and psychoanalysts are in great demand, Christian spiritual directors are simply not the fashion. There are several reasons for this. An aversion for direction may be due to a person's past experience with a dominating or incompetent director, or perhaps he feels that today all members of the Church are equal and no one should put himself forward to guide others. Balaam knew that all men are God's children but, nevertheless, all don't have the same knowledge or experience and so all can't exercise the same function in the world. He knew that all burros are equal as burros, but all don't have the speaking charism his burro had.

Some reject spiritual direction because they feel they receive enough spiritual guidance from members of a small, select Christian group or community. It is true that such membership opens them up to a rich diversity of experience and shows them a variety of possible reactions to life. But this can only help the individual in his quest for solutions to personal problems and for personal formation if it is directed and controlled by well-developed, mature persons who have these solutions to offer. Balaam would laugh at the idea that membership in some student divination club would make one capable of solving complex problems in hepatoscopy, the reading of animal livers and other entrails. He remembered the hours he passed under the guidance of his masters before he dared to read his first sheep liver. But the human heart is more complex than a sheep's liver.

Another modern objection to direction is that it implies an excessive attention to the minutiae of the spiritual life and overrefines problems by introducing subtleties and distinctions. But the same objection could be made to all developments in science, physical or social. Another charge is that the priest wastes precious time that could be better employed giving conferences to groups in greater need. But direction doesn't eliminate conferences, in which the general principles of spirituality are taught, nor does it imply that a great deal of spirituality can't be learned from books. But neither conferences nor books can supply the help an individual needs for the solution of his personal problems. Only private spiritual direction can solve these. Balak had plenty of divination handbooks on clay tablets in his royal library, but when Israel appeared at his boundary he didn't make a dash for a reference manual of omens; he sent for an expert.

Some Christians shy away from direction because they think it deforms rather than forms people and doesn't help them solve their problems, but rather makes them too dependent on someone else. They don't want to become permanent adolescents, unable to think for themselves. But a more distorted concept of direction is hardly possible. Balak had no intention of being turned into even a temporary adolescent when he sent for Balaam. The king freely chose his director to lead him to a state of spiritual autonomy, or in St. Paul's language, to make him live habitually under the Spirit's direction *(Romans 8:14)*. A director isn't the primary mover in this work. As St. John of the Cross says: "Let those who guide souls be aware and consider that the principle agent, guide and mover of souls in this work is not them, but the Holy Spirit who never ceases to care for these souls" *(Living Flame 3, 4)*. The director's job is to further God's action in the subject and to carefully avoid intruding when he isn't needed. He must guard against a *priori* ideas, practices, devotions, etc. that he may be tempted to impose on the subject.

Balaam was not only a prophet and director, but a diviner. This was a very important function in the Near Eastern world of his time, and it roughly consisted in the attempt to discern events that are distant in time or space and that consequently can't be perceived by normal means. The word divination can be used in a good sense as synonymous with the clairvoyant gifts of a prophet like Samuel who told Saul where his lost burros were to be found *(1 Samuel 9:6ff)*. Balaam didn't practice black magic but was sincerely seeking God in the circumstances of his day since the sacred text shows him living in communion with the true God, Yahweh. The divination he practiced went back to the Summerians of the third millennium, and was based on the conviction that any event may be announced or accompanied by some portent observable by man. By knowing such portents, man can foresee impending events and welcome or avert them according to their nature. Balak sent his emissaries "with the divination fee in hand" *(Numbers 22:7),* and Balaam was expected to bring along or discover a portent by which Israel's future could be foretold and controlled by a curse.

King Balak's principle was, "If you can't beat 'em, curse 'em." In the Ancient Near East, a word was no mere sound on the lips for behind it stood the soul that created it and sent it forth as an agent with a mission. Although a word backed by a weak soul had little power, one uttered by a strong soul was mighty. The spoken curse was then an active agent for harm just as a blessing was for good. As the Patriarchs blessed their children and thereby charged them with life, Balak wanted Balaam to curse his enemies and thus fill them with death. But the prophet had no intention of doing so and made it clear before leaving home. He would only speak the words God put on his lips, for both as diviner and as director he was God's instrument and nothing more.

Although Balak took extraordinary means to get the direction he needed, he didn't go as far as Saul. When this unfortunate man's spiritual guide, the prophet Samuel, died, Saul disguised himself and went by night to visit a local medium or witch at Endor to have his director called back from the grave long enough to solve the royal problem. This incident is one of the most terrifying scenes in the Bible *(1 Samuel 28:8-18),* and should be kept in mind by anyone who is tempted to exaggerate

29

the importance of the human director and forget about the principle director, the Holy Spirit *(John 16:13)*. If one's director dies or if it is impossible to find one, the Spirit will fill the need as in the case of St. Therese of Lisieux.

In the Old Testament, intimacy with God was the privilege of few. Men like Moses, Abraham, Jeremiah and Balaam enjoyed it, but the majority of men were incapable of it. The Epistle to the Hebrews, however, speaks of a new access to this intimacy under the new and definitive Alliance *(Hebrews 8:8)*, a pact that is interior and common to all: "I will place my laws in their minds and I will write them upon their hearts... and they shall not teach their fellow citizens or their brothers, saying 'Know the Lord,' for all shall know me, from least to greatest" *(Hebrews 8:10 f)*. Jesus' discourse at the Last Supper was a foreshadowing of this intimacy, and St. Paul's life and teaching are a testimony to its reality. But without an initiation through spiritual direction, most Christians will never experience it.

In spite of direction's necessity, the Christian, like Balak, must not only send for it freely, but view it as an education in freedom. This freedom is not merely tolerated but insisted upon since the purpose of direction is to reenforce or create the individual's freedom to do good. The subject must feel free to follow or set aside the director's advice, and to continue with him or leave him. Thus his actions will be the fruit of his personal appropriation of the direction received and not something imposed from without.

A Johannine text is sometimes quoted to justify rejection of spiritual direction: "As for you, the anointing you received from him remains in your hearts. This means you have no need for anyone to teach you. Rather, as his anointing teaches you about all things and is true — free from any lie — remain in him as that anointing taught you" *(1 John 2:27)*. But St. John of Avila gives the correct interpretation of this verse: "God's graces and light sometimes teach man interiorly by themselves alone, but at other times teach him both to go and ask for someone else's advice and tell him to whom he should go. In this way, the anointing teaches everything but not by itself." Balak, of course, never received this anointing but the Spirit was present in him in another way urging him to send for a director.

2

Balaam Refuses to Come

Then God came to Balaam and said, "Who are these men visiting you?" Balaam answered God, "Balak, son of Zippor, king of Moab, sent me the message: 'This people that came here from Egypt now cover the face of the earth. Please come and lay a curse on them for us; we may then be able to give them battle and drive them out." But God said to Balaam, "Do not go with them and do not curse this people, for they are blessed." The next morning Balaam arose and told the princes of Balak, "Go back to your own country, for the Lord has refused to let me go with you." So the princes of Moab went back to Balak with the report, "Balaam refused to come with us."

Balak again sent princes, who were more numerous and more distinguished than the others. On coming to Balaam they told him, "This is what Balak, son of Zippor, has to say: 'Please do not refuse to come to me. I will reward you very handsomely and will do anything you ask of me. Please come and lay a curse on this people for me.' " But Balaam replied to Balak's officials, "Even if Balak gave me his house full of silver and gold, I could not do anything, small or great, contrary to the command of the Lord, my God. But, you too shall stay here overnight, till I learn what else the Lord may tell me."

Balaam's hesitancy in answering Balak is not unusual among spiritual directors. St. John of Avila would sometimes reply immediately to letters asking his counsel, but at other times he would delay, not seeing clearly what answer to give, and would pray over the matter and say Masses to obtain light. This enabled both director and subject to be more certain that the answer came from God. As St. John says in one letter: "The Lord hasn't yet given me the answer I should give you." This delay was also common among the Desert Fathers as numerous texts attest.

After Balaam had accepted his divination stipend, in keeping with the custom of the time (cf. 1 Samuel 9:7; 1 Kings 14:3), he sought the answer he should give by sleeping in his oratory that night with the hope that God would visit him in a dream. Dream interpretation was an important branch of divination. But the text could also be understood as referring to nocturnal prayer, so it is likely that he prayed first to obtain the dream. Non-biblical contemporary texts show that this was good divination practice. For example: "Reveal yourself to me, allow me to see a favorable dream . . . may Mamu

33

the god of dreams stand near my head." God came and told his prophet that since this people were blessed, he couldn't curse them and should stay at home. Balak thought a stronger curse could annul any blessing, but Balaam refused to budge.

By his refusal, Balaam was only doing what every director must do when he sees that a meeting with a subject would either be a waste of time or positively harmful. Spiritual direction is necessary for those who are taking their first steps in the spiritual life and for anyone who has a real problem to deal with. And even those who have no special problem and are spiritually advanced will find it useful if it helps them broaden their spiritual vision and live better Christian lives. But if it is sought to satisfy the vanity of either the director or subject, or to discuss some imaginary problem, or one made up for the occasion, or out of sheer habit, it becomes useless and the director must know how to terminate it altogether.

The text shows that eventually Balaam and Balak had five or six directional interviews, for certainly more than one day was needed to move from mountain to mountain, set up altars on each, and obtain and utter an oracle. Ordinarily, at the beginning of the spiritual life, the subject will need to see his director every week or every other week. As he learns to follow the Spirit by himself, the interviews will become less frequent. At first it is good to fix a time for the next interview and urge the subject to call at that time if he needs help, since beginners often hesitate to do so. The more

34

spiritually mature will need no fixed time, since they will have the insight to call when help is required.

The interviews between the two men took place, for the most part, as they rode up and down the mountains between oracles. This was an ideal posture for direction, since it made it easy for the king to manifest his conscience. As they guided their burros and contemplated the natural beauty of the scenes unfolding below them, Balak could pour out his heart uninhibited by the violence that face-to-face contact often produces. In any directional interview the director should allow the subject to adopt the posture that suits him. Some prefer to sit side by side, others like to face the director and in some cases with some object between them such as a table with something like a flower in a pot or a bowl of goldfish on it. Many subjects like to walk during the interview; this has the advantage of softening critical moments when some traumatic personal problem is being discussed. If the subject finds the position disagreeable, he can tactfully suggest another.

Balaam and Balak were fortunate that their interview setup made it impossible for mechanization to set in. This corrosive action takes place in circumstances where the director has many subjects to care for. By scheduling interviews that are systematically restricted to a fixed number of minutes, spontaneity is squelched and the subject is made to feel like a number or a customer. While it is true that interviews should be brief, when there is no special problem to treat, every sense of haste should be eliminated or the subject will go away wondering whether he has been to a director or to a barbershop.

The main reason for Balaam's refusal to go to Moab was God's prohibition, but there may have been other reasons not mentioned in the text. The prophet's gift of clairvoyance may have led him to suspect that the king was suffering from an illusion. Such spiritual deception is quite common. Some people think every suggestion that enters their mind during prayer is from the Holy Spirit. Others imagine they have a prophetic mission. Some illusions are isolated in nature and do not affect the victim's entire life but habitual illusions do. The Desert Fathers were well acquainted with both kinds. One monk, after fifty years of heroic penance, felt inspired to throw himself into a deep pit. Another thought he was called to imitate Abraham and tried to sacrifice his own son, who fortunately escaped. A hermit from Balaam's own Mesopotamia, who surpassed all his brethren in austerity, suddenly felt called to be circumcised and to embrace Judaism. Perhaps Balaam detected an illusion of grandeur in the king. Since not long before this time the Hittite Empire under the great Suppiluliumas had extended its power over upper Mesopotamia and Syria, Balak may have been dreaming of building an empire of his own after Israel had been destroyed.

Everyone has a predominate spiritual tendency which is called his "spirit." It is a stable inclina-

tion that is usually closely related to his temperament and the evolution of his psycho-biological
organism. It can be a spirit of prayer, justice,
rebellion, austerity, poverty, etc. One spiritual
master compares it to water which takes the shape
of the vase in which it is contained. If the vase, i.e.
the nature, is good, being endowed with good
judgment, intellect and will, etc., the spirit will also
be good. A good spirit facilitates the spiritual life
while a bad one makes it difficult. The director
must be able to detect whether a spirit is good or
bad and in what manner. This reading of the spirit
is a step that precedes a reading of the promptings
it is receiving from the Holy Spirit or, as the case
may be, from evil spirits. St. Teresa of Avila was
very anxious to have St. John of Avila read her
autobiography in order to discern what kind of
spirit she had. He told her it was a good one.
Balaam, no doubt, suspected that the king of
Moab's spirit was not among the best. He waited
rightly for a clear sign from God before setting out
for Moab.

Among the spiritual director's chief tasks, the
gift of discerning spirits is one of the most difficult.
When reading spirits, it is easy to conclude from
one good or bad quality in the individual that his
whole spirit is good or bad. But this is misleading
for the whole person and the general course of his
life must be examined to see how everything
coheres or fails to cohere. Balaam may have
learned from the delegation that Balak was irasci-
ble, but he couldn't conclude from this single

feature that the king's whole spirit was bad. He had to see how this bad element fit into his whole personality before he could make a valid judgment.

Even if Balaam found that his royal subject had a defective spirit, he would try to turn it into a perfect spirit when he got to Moab. If he discovered that Balak's defects were due to weakness, ignorance, imprudence or excess, they could be corrected with relative facility, especially by means of prayer. But if the king's faults were products of his nature, it would be hard to correct them and above all if they had vitiated his nature. If he saw that the king was soaked in pride and vanity, was deceitful and given to soft living, he would do best to drop the case and spend his time more profitably with better disposed natures.

Balaam's practice of nocturnal prayer was also common among the early Christians. Hippolytus writes: "In the middle of the night, leave your bed, get up and pray. The seniors have handed on this custom to us. At this hour the whole universe rests, blessing God. The stars, trees and waters seem immobile. The entire angelic host fulfills its ministry along with the souls of the just. Thus the faithful pray at this hour" (Apos. trad. 35). The first monks made nocturnal prayer a characteristic of their life. One of their doctors, St. Basil, wrote to St. Gregory Nazianzen: "What dawn is for others, the middle of the night should be for those who practice piety, for the night's tranquility above all is agreeable to the soul, when neither eyes nor ears allow prejudicial words and sights to penetrate the heart; and the spirit, alone and recollected, unites itself to God" *(Letters 2, 6).*

After Balak had sent a bigger and better delegation to repeat his petition to the prophet, Balaam again sought an answer from God through prayer and a dream. On this night, his prayer was surely filled with intercession for all his spiritual sons, and he humbly asked God to inform him if the distant king of Moab was to become one of them. Jesus spent much of his nocturnal prayer in intercession for his disciples. St. Paul frequently mentions his prayer for his disciples *(e.g. 1 Thessalonians 1:2; 2 Timothy 1:3).* The early monks insisted that an essential function of the spiritual father was to pray for his disciples. When a monk came to a senior to place himself under his care, he gained a title to the master's prayers. Saints John of the Cross and John of Avila often refer to their prayers for the recipients of their letters of direction.

3

Balaam's Burro:
Manifestation
of Conscience

That night God came to Balaam and said to
him, "If these men have come to summon you,
you may go with them; yet only on the condition
that you do exactly as I tell you." So the next
morning when Balaam arose, he saddled his
ass, and went off with the princes of Moab.

But now the anger of God flared up at him
for going, and the angel of the Lord stationed
himself on the road to hinder him as he was
riding along on his ass, accompanied by two of
his servants. When the ass saw the angel of the
Lord standing on the road with sword drawn, she
turned off the road and went into the field, and
Balaam had to beat her to bring her back on the
road. Then the angel of the Lord took his stand
in a narrow lane between vineyards with a stone
wall on each side. When the ass saw the angel of
the Lord there, she shrank against the wall; and
since she squeezed Balaam's leg against it, he
beat her again. The angel of the Lord then went
ahead, and stopped next in a passage so narrow

that there was no room to move either to the right or to the left. When the ass saw the angel of the Lord there, she cowered under Balaam. So, in anger, he again beat the ass with his stick.

But now the Lord opened the mouth of the ass, and she asked Balaam, "What have I done to you that you should beat me these three times?" "You have acted so willfully against me," said Balaam to the ass, "that if I but had a sword at hand, I would kill you here and now." But the ass said to Balaam, "Am I not your own beast, and have you not always ridden upon me until now? Have I been in the habit of treating you this way before?" "No," replied Balaam.

Then the Lord removed the veil from Balaam's eyes so that he too saw the angel of the Lord standing on the road with sword drawn; and he fell on his knees and bowed to the ground. But the angel of the Lord said to him, "Why have you beaten your ass these three times? It is I who have come armed to hinder you because this rash journey of yours is directly opposed to me. When the ass saw me, she turned away from me these three times. If she had not turned away from me, I would have killed you; her I would have spared." Then Balaam said to the angel of the Lord, "I have sinned. Yet I did not know that you stood against me to oppose my journey. Since it has displeased you, I will go back home." But the angel of the Lord said to Balaam, "Go with the men; but you may say only what I tell you." So Balaam went on with the princes of Balak.

Numbers 22:20-35

The Lord visited his servant again and this time approved the trip to Moab. Accordingly

41

Balaam mounted his burro and set out. One of the most common forms of divination was the observation of animals' behavior. One ancient Babylonian text reads: "If an ass groans, an enemy will lay hands on its master." And another: "If a king or prince travels by chariot, and the horse on the right lies down, he will not obtain what he desires." By observing his burro's strange behavior and finally its speech, Balaam was led to see the angel and discover God's will. The burro, like the director, is only a means of helping men to know God's will and St. Augustine rightly sees in this incident an illustration of divine liberty which chooses "those whom the world considers absurd to shame the wise" *(1 Corinthians 1:27).*

The remarkable thing about this episode — which no burro lover can read without alternating feelings of pain and pleasure — is not that Balaam's burro speaks, since in legends like this speaking animals are not unusual *(cf. Genesis 3:1-5),* but that when this beast speaks it obtains a manifestation of conscience from one of the ancient world's leading spiritual guides. In spite of the beating its master had been giving it, when God granted it the gift of speech, it didn't open its mouth to curse but to question. The humble animal became the director and probed into its master's mind to discover what spirit was guiding him. Its first question suggests the unreasonableness of Balaam's conduct: "What have I done to you that you should beat me these three times?" It then appealed to their former happy relationship and the prophet's sense of justice: "Am I not your own burro, have I ever done you a mean turn before?" The animal acts like a competent director who has to be well acquainted with the subject's interior state.

An important and difficult point in the spiritual life is learning to distinguish between thoughts that come from God and those that proceed from evil spirits. The doctrine on this gift of *diacrisis* or "discernment of spirits" is ancient in the Church. It seems to be of Jewish origin, since it is found in Qumran. St. Paul knows it and in one text prays that the love of his disciples "may increase in knowledge and in all perception," so that "you may learn to value the things that really matter . . . ." *(Philippians 1:9 f).* The second century Christian work, *Shepherd of Hermas,* contains a small tract on the matter and Origen treats it at great length teaching that this gift is a charism of the highest order. The Desert Fathers consider it the art of arts, without which hermitical life especially is not safe. Stories abound on what happened to hermits who lacked it. Direction should cultivate *diacrisis* in the subject so that he can live safely in the modern desert of our secularized society. Balaam's burro showed that it knew how to exercise this gift on its master.

Since Balaam had already had spiritual direction himself, the burro rightly didn't ask for a systematic examination of the prophet's past life. But a subject who has not had previous direction should be questioned about his former spiritual

43

life, for he has had one even if it was very rudimentary. The burro took his subject as he was at present and only asked those questions necessary to solve the present problem, thus building on the work of Balaam's former directors. The director should neither demand nor admit a general confession unless the subject freely asks for it. A beginner who has never made one before may be permitted to do so, but rather than general confessions, the director should insist on a renewed spirit of contrition in every confession.

The patient burro wisely avoided making a definitive judgment on the strength of this first interview and guarded against giving Balaam the impression that it had. No subject should walk away from his opening consultation feeling that he has been classified and filed away on a card. It would mean the end of the relationship, for the subject would think the director had predestined him to react in a certain manner and so was prejudiced against him already. The director must insist that first impressions are only provisional and assure the subject that time is needed to really know him well. This will encourage him to continue his manifestation of conscience.

The burro's second question manifested confidence in the prophet's good will. It wasn't used to being beaten and knew that if Balaam would reflect on its past conduct, he would realize that there must be some serious reason for its strange behavior today. It let its master know that it thought he was a good and sincere person, in spite of the blows he had just given it. Like a good director, it let the subject know from the start that he had confidence in him. When Jesus first saw Nathanael, he remarked, "This man is a true Israelite. There is no guile in him" *(John 1:47)*. This gave the youth the confidence he needed to open his heart to Jesus. He felt that his faults would be no obstacle to their friendship and could be overcome.

The burro needed to put questions to Balaam to stimulate his manifestation of conscience, but normally the subject should not be interrupted. This is important for if the director expresses reactions to the other's statements as soon as he makes them, it will have a bad effect. Evaluative comments can inhibit the subject and produce guilt feelings. The same is true for searching questions. They make him feel he is on the carpet facing an inquisitor. And if the director interrupts with some resolution on what the subject should do now, slapping his hand on the table and crying out, "And so?" this can throw him completely off the track. Finally, the director's reactions will be especially deadly if expressed not in words but in groans or grunts.

We can only admire the little burro's self-control when Balaam has finished his manifestation. It doesn't say, "Do this or that," but waits for the angel of the Lord to open the prophet's eyes so he can see for himself why the detour was made and what should be done next. This is the right road. The subject needs time to be sure the director understands his problem before he can have confidence in his answers. And he should be made to understand that the director isn't there to hand down concrete decisions but to help him to see gradually what he should do and decide for himself. The director should not hand out bread, but yeast.

The burro saw no need to give any advice since the angel appeared to clear the matter up. But if the director sees that some counsel in the form of a suggestion will be called for, it will be good for him to first repeat the problem aloud, thus acting as a sounding board echoing the other's problems back to him. The subject is sure then that he is understood and better prepared to accept the suggestions. This also keeps the director from merely listening to the sound of his own voice instead of addressing the subject's problem directly.

The Greek Septuagint translates the burro's second question: "Haven't I been the burro upon which you have ridden since you were a youth?" This let the prophet know that his burro thought about him and had a place for him in its heart. If the subject knows that the director remembers his problem outside the interview, especially the points in it favorable to him, and ponders over it to solve it, it will increase his confidence in him. On the other hand, it is most discouraging for a subject to have to repeat very important details of his life to a director who has already heard them three or four times and has forgotten them as often.

A second millennium burro couldn't be expected to have all the psychological knowledge that modern investigation has made available to today's director. But this at least kept the good beast from using such knowledge in the wrong way or in a wrong proportion. The director's attitude must be evangelical. He is there as a representative of Christ and the Church to help this person grow in the evangelical life. If he steps out of this role to play the psychologist, he becomes just another psychologist or counsellor provided he has the competence for this work. If he doesn't have it, by continuing the interview he is simply engaging in quackery.

In this incident in his life, Balaam didn't look too good. The text shows him as an angry burro beater. We admire the burro more than him. He seems to be the real burro. The scholars tell us that this episode contains an attack on false prophets. It tells us that no matter how the word of God reaches the prophet, whether by dreams or animals' behavior, it must be accepted and obeyed. As for Balaam's conduct, we must remember that sanctity has three dimensions: a theological, by which man gives himself to God in faith and love; a moral, by which he exercises the moral virtues demanded by his conditions; and a psychological, since grace acts within the psychological circumstances of each subject. The most important dimension is the first one, if it is there and abundantly developed, the individual is a saint, even though he may be somewhat weaker on the other two dimensions. Balaam showed a little impatience and perhaps his temperament inclined him in this direction. He may be a saint who always struggled but who didn't always win. In any event, since the burro forgave him, so should we.

4

Balaam Meets Balak:
The Directional Interview

> When Balak heard that Balaam was com-
> ing, he went out to meet him at the boundary
> city Ir-Moab on the Arnon at the end of the
> Moabite territory. And he said to Balaam, "I sent
> an urgent summons to you! Why did you not
> come to me? Did you think I could not reward
> you?" Balaam answered him, "Well, I have
> come to you after all. But what power have I to
> say anything? I can speak only what God puts in
> my mouth." Then Balaam went with Balak, and
> they came to Kiriath-huzoth. Here Balak slaugh-
> tered oxen and sheep, and sent portions to
> Balaam and to the princes who were with him.
> *Numbers 22:36-40*

When Balaam finally reached Moab, his first
meeting with his new spiritual son took place in a
small frontier town, from which the king then led
him to the capital for the official reception. This
preliminary interview is important in any form of

direction. It should be a simple and affable dialogue, but like every directional meeting, the spirit of faith must keep the tone of the conversation from slipping. For artificiality, formality and superficiality can always creep in to destroy the purpose of the interview. This is especially true when the subject is a gem as unpolished as the king of Moab. Balak didn't bring the right spirit to the meeting. He was angry because his director had delayed and he immediately brought up the subject of the reward he could give him. This would be enough to break up any normal directional interview, but Balaam kept his head and let the king know that he was there to speak for God and had no interest in rewards.

In the prophet Nathan's conversation with King David *(2 Samuel 12:1-14),* we find an ideal directional interview. Nathan tells the king a clever story that awakens his sleeping conscience and causes him to condemn his own sin and do penance. As will be seen, Balaam's oracles have an analogous intention, but in this first interview the prophet will have to be satisfied with less.

The New Testament gives several examples of Jesus' directional interviews. Both Nicodemus *(John 3:1-17)* and the Samaritan woman *(John 4:6-21)* were favored with one, but the best model is in the Emmaus episode *(Luke 24:13-33).* Here Jesus intuitively opens the conversation and invites the two disciples to tell him their problem *(Luke 24:15-17).* They do so *(v. 18-24)* and Jesus lets them ramble on until they are finished, even though they bring in unnecessary details. He then reprehends them gently, reminds them of some points they had forgotten and explains the meaning of some things they already knew (v. 25-27). They immediately feel attracted to him and want him to stay (v. 29). But he conceals his humanity so their faith can pass to his invisible presence and person (v. 30-31). They follow up the interview by returning to the community they had fallen away from and enthusiastically arouse its faith (v. 32-34). Jesus didn't need any harsh language or commands to accomplish their conversion. He merely awakened the impulse hidden in their hearts and fanned it into flame so it could burn in the way he wanted. But it must be remembered that he had already known and formed these men while Balaam was faced with raw material in the king of Moab.

In a mysterious way, the Emmaus interview is repeated in every directional interview. The Risen Christ, in the person of the director, approaches a member of the Church to awaken in him and to communicate to him a deeper knowledge and love of his redeemer. As Christ's existential personification, the director manifests the same attitudes toward the subject that Jesus did while fulfilling this office on earth. These attitudes live on in the glorified Christ who communicates them through his Spirit to the person representing him in the interview. Thus spiritual direction is a mystery of initiation into union with Christ. And since Christ is most present in his Church, which the director also represents, it is an initiation into a deeper communion with the Church. Although Balaam was living under the cosmic covenant (since he was not an Israelite), the text presents him as serving Yahweh, the true God. Consequently his interview with Balak implied a presence of Yahweh in his prophet inviting the king to a more loving existence. But the Moabite wasn't disposed properly at that moment.

The directional interview isn't a sacrament, but it is a privileged moment in the Christian's life, a special participation in the mystery of the Church, the primordial sacrament of Christ, through contact with the director. It should be an encounter with Christ, parallel to that of the sacraments and it must be approached with faith. Balaam came to the interview with the right disposition, but Balak's attitude left much to be desired. He came to tell his director off rather than to manifest his conscience. He went with his mind made up and closed to anything God wanted to teach him.

The interview should initiate the subject into a filial dialogue with God and a fraternal dialogue with the Church, as represented by the director. The life of grace makes this dialogue possible, but unless Christians are initiated into it there is little hope that it will ever begin. Without this initiation most of the faithful will have only a rudimentary and formal relationship with God all their lives. Many Christians today would be delighted to live intimately with God if only someone would show them how. This is what spiritual direction should do. The negative element in Balak's attitude toward direction and its possibilities may have been attributed to earlier experience with counsellors and prophets. Perhaps he had heard nothing from them but denunciations and criticism and now that Balaam showed him there was another side to these functions, he found it hard to believe, just as many Christians today find it difficult to see a potential spiritual director in certain local priests.

Underneath all the questions and answers, doctrinal explanations and manifestations of personal problems that every interview implies, a real living word of God that envelops and sanctifies the whole conversation is being spoken. An interior conversation is taking place between God and the two individuals as well as the exterior exchange of words between the director and subject. With his human limitations, the director is trying to listen to God as well as to the subject. He is attempting to understand and repeat God's word to the Christian sitting before him who isn't yet perfectly docile to it. This was clear in the opening interview in Moab. The king was far from docile to God's message, but the counsellor had his ear to the ground trying to catch every syllable and repeat it to his subject.

The directional interview is then primarily intended for those who don't know yet how to detect and listen to God's voice. Like the boy Samuel, they need someone to help them recognize it *(1 Samuel 3)*. God speaks to every human heart in many ways, but most men don't know how to distinguish this voice. Like Jesus, then, the director must go especially to the spiritually hard of hearing and the spiritually sick. Balaam knew he was answering a sick call when he set out for Moab. This king was not only spiritually deaf, but was passing through a crisis severe enough to cause even the spiritually healthy and mature to call for help.

The Epistle to the Hebrews teaches: "God's word is living and effective, sharper than any two-edged sword. It penetrates and divides soul and spirit, joints and marrow; it judges the reflections and thoughts of the heart" (Hebrews 4:12). Balaam never heard this text but from experience with that word he knew he wasn't wasting time by speaking it even to a tough specimen like Balak. He knew it would do something to the king. It wouldn't leave him alone but, as St. John of Avila says, would agitate him interiorly more than the strongest rhubarb. He wouldn't leave the interview unchanged. No one who exposes himself to that word will be able to continue in spiritual sloth, vanity, envy or any other vice because God's word will keep coming back to him to remind him of his evil conduct. It will visit him as the angel of the Lord visited Balaam to instruct and correct him; or as a doctor on a house call will cure the ailments the patient manifests to him. So the spiritual director will try to heal whatever spiritual illness the subject freely exposes.

When Balaam responded so calmly to Balak's

gruff opening remarks, he showed that he had the serenity a director needs. By rejecting rewards, he manifested another essential quality: incorruptibility. He knew that sometimes it is best to momentarily overlook a subject's fault in order to be better able to correct it later on, but his respect for the exigencies of God and for the dignity of the spiritual life was too great to allow him to wink at the king's voluntary weakness. He insisted that Balak comply with the demands of God's word and spoke frankly, even at the risk of seeing Balak reject his direction and look for a new counsellor. Every good director will suffer defections, just as Jesus did, and will let the subject go without reproaches and with his prayers, for after all another guide may do more good in this case. Woe to the director who begins to think that only his spiritual detergent really gets souls white!

Balaam was firm with Balak, but never severe — two very different things. Jesus was often firm with St. Peter, but severe only once — when he had to tell him, "Get out of my sight, you satan!" *(Matthew 16:23)*. In acting firmly, the director must be careful to temper this with charity and discretion. Even when he has to tell a subject how reasonable it would be for him to look for another guide, he must do so in a way that makes it clear that personal resentment is absent from his decision. And of course the subject who leaves must do all he can to be sure that the same sort of reasons aren't motivating his departure.

The Desert Fathers condemn the rare cases of

severity practiced among them in direction. The spiritual father who discouraged rather than animated his subjects was unworthy of his office. They knew that no one is really changed by harshness, for one devil isn't cast out by another. When the priest ordered a certain brother who had sinned to leave the assembly, one of the community directors got up and went out with him saying, "I too am a sinner." This is why Balaam didn't utter a single harsh word to the king throughout their relationship. His closing oracle, however, contained a prediction of Moab's defeat at Israel's hands, for even the great St. Anthony couldn't tolerate hardness of heart and answered a brother who asked for his prayers, "Neither I nor God will have mercy on you, if you don't get to work earnestly especially by praying."

All the sacraments are an encounter with Christ, but since all don't contain a real dialogue, all aren't an interview with Christ. A directional interview can often be combined with a sacrament, when the director applies the doctrine of the particular sacrament to the subject. This is easy to do in confession, since an interview is part of the sacrament. Both direction and confession depend upon a manifestation of conscience, but in confession this touches only the sins committed while in direction personal dispositions are also brought up. The sacrament operates *ex opere operato,* while direction's efficacy is dependent on the director's ability. When the two are combined, direction can help the subject make a more fruitful confession, reconciling him to God with more love and generosity as well as promoting the secondary effects of this reconciliation, such as peace and consolation. Balak of course lived before the sacraments of the New Law were instituted, but his disposition at that moment would have excluded him from sacramental graces just as it did from those of direction.

Balak gave Balaam more opportunities than this first interview to prove his competence as a director. And even when he was dissatisfied with him after the first oracle, he still gave him more chances. A subject may find that his director is unconsciously leading him into useless conversations, a sensual friendship or some practices contrary to his vocation. Or he may simply feel that this man or woman is not adapted to his particular situation or not really interested in his spiritual progress. These would be sufficient motives for looking around for another guide. But if the new director is sought because he happens to be popular at the moment, or for some other human motive, it would be better to stay put. Like Balak, some subjects wouldn't be improved by an Elijah or a John the Baptizer.

No human being is ever going to have all the qualities needed for an ideal spiritual director. So no list of such qualifications should make those called to this office back away from it, nor should it cause those looking for a director to despair of ever finding one. God's power operates through human weakness when that weakness is humble and trustful. Balaam certainly didn't have all the qualities that the perfect director should have, but he had the main ones.

First, Balaam's doctrinal preparation was adequate for those days and kept up to date, since he was famous for his skill throughout the Near East. He was also a good psychologist, as is clear from the way he handled the king of Moab. His general culture was broad enough to enable him to converse reasonably well on a considerable number of topics related to his work, otherwise no king would have invited him to his court. He was a man of realistic and sound judgment, not easily startled or panicked, as the incident with his talking burro shows. He had enough leadership to keep those he was trying to help from pulling him along with them. His spirit of faith was so deeply rooted that it survived the loss of a high position at court. He manifested great affective maturity when he concluded his interview with the king on a note of triumph rather than depression in spite of its failure. He had enough light to penetrate men's hearts and could communicate easily with them. We don't know enough about his private life to be able to say that he preached more by example than by word, but we are sure that he could inspire confidence and open hearts.

Balaam certainly knew how to accommodate himself to others, and the text shows how he kept his role as director subordinate to that of the Spirit. He didn't permit any theatrics to slip into his interviews. He didn't change staffs into snakes to impress subjects like the Egyptian magicians did (Ex-

odus 7:11). He was very tactful and wasn't the cerebral sort who tenaciously cling to their views in the face of more experienced persons. Although he knew how to conduct a conversation, he could hardly be up on our modern insights into this art. He kept the secrets that emerged in the course of his work and was gifted with a sense of humor sound enough to keep him from reaching for the rope, like Ahithophel *(cf. 2 Samuel 16:23),* when he saw that his counsel wasn't followed. Balaam then did what he could with the qualities he had and this is all God or any subject can expect from any director.

Jesus' example shows us how important an affable manner is in direction. When Philip brings Nathanael to meet him, Our Lord overcomes his resistance with the remark, "Before Philip called you, I saw you under the fig tree" *(John 1:48).* This statement is an exegetical nut that will always remain uncracked. It refers to some secret detail in Nathanael's life that made him realize that Jesus knew and loved him. It opened his heart at once. Balaam had no such secret detail to throw at the king on their first meeting, but Balak would have let it pass as just another magic trick of this foreign soothsayer.

Jesus' personal goodness also attracted the rich young man who ran up and asked about eternal life. When Our Lord told him what he must do, the youth requested further direction. Before answering, "Jesus looked at him with love" *(Mark 10:21)* and because he loved him, he invited him to follow him. This is how someone looking for direction will find a director. He will be attracted by the goodness he sees and draw near. The director must be sure to meet him with Jesus' attitude and see that this affability forms the atmosphere of the interviews. Balaam brought plenty of personal goodness to Moab, but Balak's aggressive arrogance in this first meeting made the director's position a painful one.

All we know about Balak is what this story tells us, but we have some details about a few of his kingly successors. King Eglon, for example, who the sacred text says was "very fat," oppressed the Israelites soon after they entered Canaan. He was detested by them and God raised up a Benjaminite named Ehud to assassinate him. The story forms one of the Bible's best murder tales and could be entitled "The Case of the Vanishing Dagger." Ehud was left-handed and hid a dagger a foot long at his right thigh. He brought the Israelite tribute to the king and then requested a private audience. When he was alone with Eglon:

> Ehud went in to him where he sat alone in his cool upper room (and) said, "I have a message from God for you." So the king rose from his chair, and Ehud with his left hand drew the dagger from his right thigh, and thrust it into Eglon's belly. The hilt also went in after the blade, and the fat closed over the blade because he did not withdraw the dagger from his body. Then Ehud went out into the hall, shutting the doors of the upper room on him and locking them. . . .
>
> *Judges 3:19-23*

The fat closed on the dagger locking it in and then the doors closed on the dead king locking him in his room. If King Balak was anything like King Eglon, it is easy to understand how Balaam's affability would have been wasted on him.

The director's goodness must be authentic and his affability sincere, but this must not be a response to the subject's natural qualities. A subject won't find the security he seeks, if he realizes his director is impressed by his human qualities. After all, he didn't come to direction looking for admiration. He must feel that the director's goodness is that of a man of God toward someone in spiritual need. Then he can see God in the director and his goodness as a reflection of God's. But Balak wasn't even interested in admirers, he wanted someone who could curse.

The affable atmosphere of the directional interview anticipates man's glorified state, when the flesh will follow the spirit without resistance. But in our present state the director will often have to force his smile; yet this must be done, for his kindness will create an atmosphere of equality that will make the subject feel that the director's time and talents are placed at his disposal without condescension. Balak never suspected his director of condescension. Balaam's problem was to be kind without allowing his subject to dominate him.

The text gives no indication that Balaam was in a hurry to get rid of the king. He didn't yawn, close his eyes or look bored. He seems to have had nothing else to do except listen to the king's problem. If the subject feels that he is boring the director, it gives him the impression that his spiritual life isn't important to him. The director must never be in a hurry and must listen in imitation of God, who is ever attentive to the prayers and needs of his children. He must listen lovingly and patiently, not only trying to catch everything the subject says, but also the things he is afraid to say and only hints at.

While Balak poured out his troubles to the prophet, Balaam didn't listen like a stone wall; he explained some of his difficulties to the king. He told him his hands were tied by the Lord and that no matter how much he wanted to help him, he could only speak what the Lord permitted. He didn't act then like a passive recipient of Balak's pronouncement, but prudently contributed his own. He didn't tell the king everything that was on his mind. This would have been uncharitable as well as imprudent, since the interview's purpose was to settle the king's problem and not his own. But Balaam knew how to answer questions by imbuing his answers with a personal touch that made the truth seem to flow from personal experience. Every director should be able to communicate enough of his own experience to make the subject feel not only understood but in the presence of a fellow traveler.

Balaam was summoned to help Balak, but the Desert Fathers sometimes went uncalled to visit those in spiritual need. St. Macarius of Egypt learned that a certain hermit was in spiritual straights and set out to visit him. "How are things going?" he asked. The hermit dissimulated by answering with a monastic formula, "Fine, thanks to your prayers." Macarius then asked, "Do you have any trouble with bad thoughts?" The younger monk slipped out of this too by saying, "So far, all is going well." Macarius then opened his heart. "Look, my son, I've been practicing renunciation for many long years and am held in honor by all, and yet, in spite of being an old man, the demon of lust still torments me." This broke the ice and the hermit said, "Believe me, father, he torments me too." Macarius then proceeded to tell him all his other temptations until he had provoked a complete confession.

Balaam, fortunately, avoided one of the director's worst mistakes: talking over the subject's head. He brought his conversation down to the king's low spiritual level without trying to utopistically raise him to the mystical life on the first day. Like St. Paul with the Thessalonians, he was "gentle as any nursing mother fondling her little ones" *(1 Thessalonians 2:7)*. This called for real renunciation on Balaam's part, but otherwise Balak would have had to practice self-denial as he listened to some lofty spiritual discourse that to him was just so much gop.

The text tells us that Balak conducted his guest to the capital where the official reception was held. Part of this consisted in sacrifices, but there was no doubt some kind of banquet or ball of reception held afterward. This was customary in those times *(Genesis 18:6-8; 1 Samuel 9:23 f)*,

63

and it shows Balak's respect for his guest in spite of his anger. We can be sure Balaam reciprocated. He didn't consider the king just another case he would have to occupy his mind with during the interview, but carried the problem with him and prayed over it. Every director will want to be more than an occasional advisor for his subjects. He will want to develop a relationship that will avoid forming too close a familiarity but will become a real friendship nevertheless.

Balaam and Balak didn't become friends but when direction goes on for months or years real affection can spring up. Neither party should be surprised, for direction could hardly be profitable if there were no mutual esteem. The fact should be faced and kept in its place. This is a chance for the director especially to exercise his affective maturity.

The director-subject relationship, like other dual relationships such as father-son, husband-wife and master-disciple, sets in motion a special affective dynamism which creates intense affective possibilities. But this relationship, unlike the husband-wife union, isn't exclusive because it lies in the spiritual order and thus is capable of multiplication. Due to his chastity, the director can multiply this relationship and still preserve its dual character. He can have many spiritual sons and daughters each regarding him as their father. Balaam and Balak soon realized that each was made for other dual relationships and not this one.

Perhaps Balak was one of those unfortunate

individuals who never had a spiritual father. He was a spiritual orphan who grew up with no initiation into the spiritual life. The spiritual life, like all life, is transmitted by paternity; and the affective relation between director and subject is essential to this paternity and healthy. If a Christian has never experienced it, his affective life will remain imperfectly developed. But the psychological term "affective transference" should not be attached to this relationship. This tag should be reserved for cases in which some other dual relationships that haven't been realized in the person or were frustrated are mixed in with the directional relationship. These are real affective transferences and they can destroy the director-subject relationship. Their causes must be sought in the affective background of either party, or attributed to the awakening of other dual tendencies proper to everyone that now appear and set about disturbing or dominating the directional relationship; for since this relationship creates a privileged situation, these parasite tendencies can easily creep in. If Balak had begun to see a father or an uncle in Balaam, an unhealthy and true affective transference would have taken place.

We can't be sure if Balak ever experienced any psychological complications in direction. These arise because the subject becomes in some way a child in regard to the director, asking questions and solutions and seeking formation. It is hard to imagine the king of Moab adopting such an attitude. So he may never have known the interferences that identification and ambivalence can bring to direction. When these appear, both parties must struggle to keep the paternity proper to direction predominate and healthy so that it can suffocate any parasitic affections. If the director, above all, is well integrated affectively he will overcome the crisis after identifying it and preserve the relationship from shipwreck.

It isn't likely that Balaam himself fell victim to an affective interference. But if the director does find that he is suffering from an affective disorder, it is normally best to discreetly but firmly break off the relationship for there is small chance that he will be able to completely get rid of his affection, especially if the subject is a woman.

Perhaps the best explanation for Balak's anger during the first interview lies in a psychological transference. If he projected the image of his father onto Balaam, and if he had a problem with his father, then it becomes easier to see why he exploded. We only know that the king's father was named Zippor, which means "bird" or "sparrow." Perhaps he was too authoritative and didn't believe in dialogue. The young Balak may have suffered keenly and as a result unconsciously saw him again in Balaam. This kind of transference is especially unalterable. It doesn't like to be cleared up and insists that it acts in good faith. It is bipolar, i.e. aggressive, and yet claims to be ready to do all the director asks. If the subject is aware that this can happen, it will be easier for him to prevent it. Once the director has spotted it, he must not play with it, but eliminate it by making the subject stick to facts and by exposing the subjectivity of his explanation of those facts.

Besides projecting his father onto Balaam the king may have seen some other figure in the prophet. Perhaps he identified him with a king to whom he owed tribute, and so he would constantly feel a need to justify himself before him. Or he may have seen some benevolent minor god in Balaam which could deliver him from every evil, and this would lead him to try to please the prophet in order to get favors from him. Maybe he projected the image of his mother onto his counsellor and so looked to him for all his decisions. No one engaged in a directional relationship is guaranteed immunity from these psychological mechanisms, but a good director will recognize and control them.

Without *cardiognosis,* the gift of reading hearts, Balaam could not have become so prominent in his profession. No direction is possible if the director doesn't have some share in this charism. If, after several interviews, a subject still feels that the director doesn't understand him, he should look for another guide. No director can be expected to read a subject as if he were an open book, but he should be able to pick up what he is saying when it has been expressed clearly enough. Perfect understanding from a director is not possible. St. Teresa said she spent twenty years without finding a director who understood her *(Life, ch. 4).* But if long explanations about one's intentions, temptations, etc. are necessary, it is time to change directors. This was Balak's conclusion after several interviews with his imported guide.

Self-purification and self-knowledge are the best preparation for learning to read other men's hearts. As St. John of the Cross says, those who "have a purged spirit are naturally able to know with great facility — some better than others — what is hidden in the heart and spirit of others as well as their inclinations and talents. They can do so by means of exterior indications, even very small ones, such as words, movements and other signs" *(Ascent 2, 26, 14)*. We don't know if Balaam had this gift of psychic radiography in as high a degree as St. Paul the Simple who could simply look at people as they came into church and give an account of their thoughts. This charism, also called *diórasis,* gives a second sight to its possessor by which he can penetrate matter, time and space. Among the Desert Fathers it was more rare than *diacrisis,* or discernment of spirits. The best directors had both charisms.

The secret of disposing a subject for an easy manifestation of conscience is to help him see the director as another self. Then he will open his heart as if talking to himself, or rather to someone who is another self in addition to being kind, balanced, wise and able to supply what he lacks; to someone who understands him better than he does himself, and judges him with more mercy than he could bestow on himself. Then his manifestation will flow like the waters of Siloah in peace and tranquility. If

68

this was impossible in this first interview with the king, perhaps later at the reception ball when his majesty was in better spirits Balaam received more than one earful of royal secrets.

No competent director will think that being benevolent means approving of everything a subject says or taking his every word as gold that needs no refining. Balaam frankly but kindly contradicted the king. But he also carefully avoided a suspicious attitude toward him, for there is nothing more deadly to spiritual direction. It inhibits any manifestation of conscience and so makes profit from the interview impossible. Balaam therefore tried to make his subject feel that he was there to make contact with his hidden goodness and to develop it to the fullest.

5

The Oracles:
The Art of Suggestion

When the reception ball was over and Balaam reached his private quarters, he reflected on his situation. He knew that his task was to let the king see that Israel was here to stay because Yahweh was protecting it. Consequently he would have to help him face this new world and find his place in it. He would have to guide him in the formation of a sound conscience, a balanced self-judgment, a sense of moderation and personal initiative in his spiritual life. In addition he would have to lead him to a new relationship with God by prayer, with himself by self-denial and with other men by fraternal charity. But if he put such a program bluntly to Balak, it would be counterproductive. There was only one thing to do then: resort to suggestion. This was what he planned to do by means of his oracles, his *mashalim*. The art of suggestion is a key to fruitful spiritual direction, and Balaam gives us some excellent examples of its practice.

Jesus used parables to suggest things to his audiences, but he had other means too. In many cases he acted by suggestion not only because his hearers were unprepared for his teaching, but because spiritual guidance is given better by suggestion and reminder than by command and exhortation. This is how the Spirit operates: "He will instruct you in everything and remind you of all that I told you" *(John 14:26)*. This procedure is only possible if there is spiritual fervor in the subject. Balak had this to some degree, especially after his first interview and his chat with his director at the reception ball.

Every norm given in an imperative or exhortative tone is always felt to be an external principle or an impulse from without. By nature it implies that the subject needs to be spurred on rather than held back because he is so low in interior energy. But suggestion stimulates the subject's immanent activity, which is the goal of spiritual direction. "All who are led by the Spirit of God are sons of God" *(Romans 8:14)*. Balak lived before the great outpouring of that Spirit, but it was present in him in another way urging him to obey the truth. By acting through suggestion, Balaam was echoing and supporting God's voice within the king.

Balaam hoped his suggestions would affect the king in much the same way as the sight of a bale of hay affected his remarkable burro. By simply displaying it to the beast, its appetite was aroused and it moved toward it with no need of a command or exhortation. The king's spark of fervor had to be blown into flame by Balaam's suggestions so that it spontaneously burned in the right direction. His action remained immanent, although correlated with the director's authority, for Balak freely consented to that authority when he made Balaam his director. By acting in this way, the prophet also showed the king his confidence in his fervor and good intentions.

Suggestion thus acts like a fecundating rain on the seed of God's word hidden within every believer's heart, causing it to come to life and bear fruit. The Spirit from within and the director from without cooperate in making the subject a better child of God, doing in complete freedom what pleases its Father because it pleases him. Although this policy didn't produce full fruit in Balak, the text proves that it did affect the king for the better for his response to the first oracle was anger *(Numbers 23:11)*, but to the second he reacted with a mitigated compromise *(Numbers 23:25)*. If the third provoked a new explosion of wrath *(Numbers 24:10)*, his final response was silence *(Numbers 24:25)*. God's grace may have finally won out.

Balaam had as many forms of suggestion to choose from as Jesus did. For example, at times Our Lord used a simple indication, as with the rich young man. "If you seek perfection, go, sell your possessions . . . come back and follow me" *(Matthew 19:21)*. This wasn't an exhortation or an order, but a simple pointing to the way. It created a crisis in the youth's heart because he wanted to follow Jesus but keep his wealth. The money won out and he left sad and no longer interested in direction. Jesus let him go without a word. The mother of Jesus used the same form at Cana: "They have no more wine" *(John 2:3)*.

An open question can serve the same purpose. Thus Jesus asked his parents, "Why did you search for me? Did you not know I had to be in my Father's house?" *(Luke 2:49)*. This was a hint that they should reflect on the nature of his mission. He also used hanging questions, "What, then, if you were to see the Son of Man ascend to where he was before...?" *(John 6:62)*. Balaam could have put this sort of question to Balak, "What if you were to start loving Israel...?" But he chose a different form.

When dealing with very sensitive cases, the abstract statement is an especially effective form. Jesus used it on Nicodemus, "No one can enter God's kingdom without being begotten of water and Spirit" *(John 3:5)*. Even though a subject may have asked his director to pull no punches with him, when the truth touches a highly sensitive wound, a violent reflex-reaction can take place, even against his will. By using an abstract statement, the blow is softened for it acts as the major premise of a syllogism and leaves the subject to apply it to his own case. But Balaam had an even better form of suggestion for Balak.

The best form of suggestion is one that doesn't use words, at least formal words, but deeds. For example, Jesus taught the law of self-

73

denial best by taking up his cross. And the best way for Balaam to show the king that Israel must be loved was by blessing it. This is what he did.

The sacred text only gives us the oracles and their immediate setting with sacrifices and dialogue. It thus forces us to fill in what happened while Balak successively led his director to three different mountain ridges, which happened to be the sites of the region's three most famous pagan sanctuaries: Bamoth-Baal, Nebo or Pisgah and Baal-Peor. The directional interviews were held during these rides through the mountains. It was then that Balaam helped the king understand his special charism, i.e. the stable service for which God had endowed him and that he could render to others in the new situation being formed by Israel's presence.

The discovery of Balak's charism involved two steps: first, the exploration of his aptitudes; and second, the identification of the spirit urging him to exercise these aptitudes. For St. Paul makes it clear that it is essential in dealing with charisms to find out if they spring from love and are exercised under its impulse *(1 Corinthians 12 & 13)*. This is also a guarantee of their authenticity. The director's primary task is to see whether or not his subject has a loving spirit. At times he may also help him recognize his aptitudes. Balaam could see that Balak was mainly motivated by the spirit of Cain.

Saints Paul and John give doctrinal soundness as one indication of a good spirit. An authentic charism won't inspire its possessor to deny revealed teaching *(Romans 12:6; 2 Timothy 3:13 ff)*. As a polytheist, Balak's spirit could be judged by its conformity with the law God has inscribed in every heart. But even by this standard, he would be found wanting.

In addition to the criteria listed by St. Paul in his hymn to charity *(1 Corinthians 13),* one of the surest signs of a spirit moved by God is humility, the lack of a spirit of total self-sufficiency. When God's Spirit moves an individual to some task, it inspires a humble tension toward it. The person is aware of his dependence on God and of his own incapacity. A charismatic individual is always ready to listen to the Spirit and to other people. Balak would only listen as long as he heard what he wanted to hear.

A possessive attitude toward a gift — viewing it as a personal trophy or baseball bat to beat others over the head with — is a clear sign of a pseudo-charism. A true charism is a responsibility, a gift that leads the individual to go out of himself rather than to seek his own interest. The Holy Spirit never inspires an attitude of radical rebellion, resentment or hatred. An a priori posture of opposition to others and a lack of humble, intelligent collaboration such as we find in the king of Moab indicate a bad spirit.

In his oracles Balaam intended to include a gentle suggestion that just as God has chosen Israel and given it a special task in the world, so too he must have some particular work for which he had chosen and endowed Balak. And just as God was protecting Israel in the fulfillment of its charism, so too he would extend his aid to Balak, if the king would cooperate. But unfortunately the shadow of Cain, the fugitive, had already fallen over the land of Moab and darkened the king's spiritual vision.

Balaam's oracles were the first part of his story to be given an exact form by tradition. The Israelite historians preserved most of the literary structure of these poems, which was comparable to that used by Sumo-Akkadian diviners, but drained them of their astrological and magical elements. The four major oracles, alike in vocabulary and style, were carried by two different traditions. The third and fourth belong to the Yahwist, the first and second to the Elohist tradition. Each school interpreted them in the light of its own theology. The Yahwist used its oracles especially to predict a glorious future for the house of David, since it reinterpreted them during David's or Solomon's lifetime. The Elohist, writing in the first half of the eighth century, employed its two poems for more spiritual and less nationalistic ends, stressing Israel's religious mission in the world. By adapting them to contemporary situations, their rich spiritual message was kept alive. We must read them today in the light of the New Covenant.

6

The First Oracle:
Formation in Prayer

Next morning Balak took Balaam and
brought him up to Bamoth-baal, from where he
could see the end of the camp. Balaam said to
Balak, 'Build me seven altars, and bring here to
me seven bulls and seven rams.' Balak did as
Balaam asked and he offered a holocaust of one
bull and one ram on each altar. Balaam then said
to Balak, 'Stand beside your holocausts. I will
go; perhaps Yahweh will allow me to meet him.
Whatever he shows me I shall tell you.' And he
withdrew to a bare hill.

The oracles of Balaam

God came to meet Balaam, who said to
him, 'I have prepared the seven altars and offered a holocaust of one bull and one ram on
each altar.' Yahweh then put a word into his
mouth and said to him, 'Go back to Balak and
that is what you must say to him.' So Balaam
went back to him, and found him still standing
beside his holocaust, with all the chiefs of Moab.
Then he declaimed his poem. He said:

> 'Balak brought me from Aram,
> the king of Moab from the hills of Kedem,
> "Come, curse Jacob for me;
> come, denounce Israel."
> How shall I curse one when God does not
>   curse?
> How shall I denounce when God does not
>   denounce?
> Yes, from the top of the crags I see him,
> from the hills I observe him.
> See, a people dwelling apart,
> not reckoned among the nations.
> Who can count the dust of Jacob?
> Who can number the cloud of Israel?
> May I die the death of the just!
> May my end be one with theirs!'
>
> Balak said to Balaam, 'What have you done
> to me? I brought you to curse my enemies, and
> you heap blessings on them!' Balaam answered,
> 'Am I not obliged to say what Yahweh puts into
> my mouth?'
>
> *Numbers 22:41-23:12*

The next morning as they rode up the slopes of Bamoth-baal, Balaam decided to begin his spiritual education of the king by initiating him into a new life of prayer. He first asked Balak what kind of prayer he had been practicing, so that he could lead him further along the road that had already proved fruitful. For a director must never impose his own style of prayer on a subject but respect whatever form the other is using as long as there are no mistakes being made.

The prophet saw at once that Balak wasn't too well along in his prayer life. He was still on all fours. The king proudly told him that he was a real bear for liturgical ceremonies, and therefore had a deep life of prayer. Balaam had to point out that liturgical prayer is only a part of that life and not its whole substance. Balaam wanted the king to learn to breathe before God, to live with him all day long. He couldn't tell him, however, that there is a reality called mental prayer, something so delicate that no method can ever entirely succeed in leading man into it. For it is a vital contact with God, and as every vital encounter, it can't be programmed or reduced to rules that always work. A living encounter with another person is always contingent, for persons are mysteries of freedom. Sometimes one thing will happen, sometimes something else. Man will find God with peace and joy in prayer at times, but at other times he will seem to be standing before a closed door.

The two men were still talking about prayer when they reached the summit, and preparation for the oracle began. The first step was the customary sacrifices. Some diviners used eight but Balaam settled for seven. Balak was efficient at liturgical matters and felt that the more expensive and numerous the sacrifices, the greater the potency of the coming curse. Balaam however regarded them as a form of intercessory prayer to obtain a vision and a word from God. As soon as the animals had been offered, the prophet, like an even greater spiritual director and intercessor, Moses, went alone to meet God. He didn't seek contact with God through magic but through mystical prayer.

When God arrived and gave him his word, he returned to the king and pronounced it. He didn't despise the methods and preparations for obtaining contact with God that were in use at that time, but neither did he rely on them or believe they caused the contact.

Balaam may have looked down at Israel and seen a cloud of dust rising from their camp *(Numbers 23:10)* and interpreted it with the inspired word he had just received from God. His oracle first repeated the classical doctrine that no one can curse against God's will. Then, rather than an explicit blessing, he merely repeated the ancient blessings of Abraham and Jacob *(Genesis 13:16; 15:15; 28:14)* in which they were promised a numerous posterity. The prophet next recalled Israel's separation from other nations as God's own people, and expressed the desire that he, a gentile, might share their lot by participating in their blessing. Christian tradition sees this oracle fulfilled in the new spiritual Israel, not separated by circumcision, but by faith in Christ whose members die in an enviable way since they "die in the Lord" *(Revelation 14:13).*

As might be expected, Balak was enraged but as it was getting late, he decided to be a good sport and give the prophet a new look at Israel tomorrow. As they descended from the mountain, Balaam explained to the king that there are two kinds of prayer. One is solemn and formal and more proper to the liturgy, but the other is a real familiarity with God. St. Paul knows both. Many liturgical prayers are mixed into his epistles, but they also show that their author lived in deep familiarity with Christ. He says at one point, "Three times I begged the Lord that this might leave me" *(2 Corinthians 12:8)* referring to his infirmity. The Greek original "to beg or beseech" indicates a type of asking for things common among friends. Both forms of prayer assist each other, for liturgical prayer is directed to the Father through Jesus and familiar prayer to Jesus springs from this filial relation to the Father that Jesus has made possible for us and vivifies it.

If Balaam had suggested mental prayer to the king, his majesty would have taken the same violent approach to it that he took to everything else. He would have tried to concentrate by nervous and muscular force and would have found it hard to believe that the basic attitude in all mental prayer is a simple opening of the heart to God's action, peacefully allowing all created things to fall from the mind so that it can spontaneously rise to God. Nervous tension of any kind shows that there is something artificial and forced about the prayer.

Balak could understand how man can think about God for a while, but this isn't prayer. We can come away from time spent speculating about God feeling pleased with ourselves for having had such sublime thoughts, but real prayer always makes us more humble and aware of our misery and our need of God.

It is impossible to say whether Balak would have been interested in some of the forms of concentration popular today — such as the oriental methods or transcendental meditation. His director would certainly have had a serene and prudent attitude toward them. He would not have been carried away with enthusiasm nor by a desire for novelty, nor by an urge to keep up with the spiritual Joneses; nor would he have refused to use them and explain them to his subjects when they proved really helpful. But like all methodical exercises, they should be filled with a Christian spirit and practiced therefore with diligence but without putting too much trust in them, for our confidence can only rest in the Lord.

Beyond any doubt Balak would have understood and admired a modern charismatic community, since such groups were known in a primitive form in the Ancient Near East *(cf. 1 Samuel 10:5ff; 19:18 ff)*. He would probably not have joined one, however, because although they often have a moderator who preserves order in the progression of the community prayer, he isn't a real director of the meeting; and it is hard to believe that the king of Moab would have prayed on an equal footing with everyone else as is common in these communities.

A director may be asked about a charismatic community or may see that he should suggest that the subject join one. He should advise him then to keep an eye on his experiences during the meetings because such gatherings can create an atmosphere in which certain forms of hysteria can break out to spoil fruit that is usually to be gathered from these meetings. The moderators must make sure that nothing enters in that doesn't bear the marks of the Spirit. Such communities have helped many Christians to discover what prayer can mean in their lives and have become the starting point for general spiritual growth. They must never be turned into absolute ends, however, but should be used as incentives to a closer union with Christ and a better service of others. Balak would have needed a stronger experience than can be found in the charismatic movement to make prayer a personal reality for him.

Balaam had one last hope that might lead Balak into a life of prayer: vocal prayer. Christians must never lose their esteem for this kind of prayer. Many persons, especially the more extroverted — such as St. Anthony Claret, for example — find it the easiest and most natural form of prayer, even at the end of their spiritual development. It shouldn't be regarded as exclusively for beginners. A full life of prayer will contain doses of it every day.

No matter what form of concentration or prayer one uses, it must never be a substitute for the basic biblical preparation for prayer which is purity of heart. This is a deep desire to please God in everything, to live free from bad thoughts and in the constant memory of him. The early monks recognized its importance, but none more than Cassian for whom purity of heart was identical with charity. For him the heart was the spirit, the most noble and vital part of man, the principle of intuitive knowledge which when free from evil passions, puts man in direct contact with God and makes him docile to his action. But how could Balaam teach purity of heart to a Moabite whose heart was like the heart of Cain?

This oracle shows us that Balaam was not only a man of prayer, but a visionary. According to the Bible, a vision is an insight into the hidden reality surrounding man and an unfolding of the concealed future. Balaam had one vision after his burro began to speak. God opened his eyes so he could see the angel on the road just as he opened the eyes of Elisha's servant to see "the mountainside filled with horses and fiery chariots around Elisha" *(2 Kings 6:17)*. But the prophet's greatest visions were on the mountain tops. In these he left us the best and most detailed visionary descriptions in the Old Testament. They can be an indication of God's presence in the seer although by themselves, as St. John of the Cross teaches, they aren't worth the least act of humility *(Ascent 3, 9, 4)*.

7

The Second Oracle: Formation in Self-Denial

Then Balak said to him, "Please come with me to another place from which you can see only some and not all of them, and from there curse them for me." So he brought them to the lookout field on the top of Pisgah, where he built seven altars and offered a bullock and a ram on each of them. Balaam then said to Balak, "Stand here by your holocaust, while I seek a meeting over there." Then the Lord met Balaam, and having put an utterance in his mouth, he said to him, "Go back to Balak, and speak accordingly." So he went back to Balak, who was still standing by his holocaust together with the princes of Moab. When Balak asked him, "What did the Lord say?" Balaam gave voice to his oracle:

Be aroused, O Balak, and hearken;
give ear to my testimony, O son of Zippor!
God is not man that he should speak
*   falsely,*
nor human, that he should change his

mind.
Is he one to speak and not act,
to decree and not fulfill?
It is a blessing I have been given to
pronounce;
a blessing which I cannot restrain.
Misfortune is not observed in Jacob,
nor misery seen in Israel.
The Lord, his God, who brought him out
of Egypt,
a wild bull of towering might.
No, there is no sorcery against Jacob,
nor omen against Israel.
It shall yet be said of Jacob,
and of Israel, "Behold what God has
wrought!"
Here is a people that springs up like a
lioness,
and stalks forth like a lion;
It rests not till it has devoured its prey
and has drunk the blood of the slain.

"Even though you cannot curse them," said
Balak to Balaam, "at least do not bless them."
But Balaam answered Balak, "Did I not warn
you that I must do all that the Lord tells me?"
Numbers 23:13-26

Balak didn't give up after his first attempt and
on the morning of the next day we see the little
group ascending Pisgah, the last ridge of the
slopes of Mt. Nebo, a spot favored by a monastery
during the Christian era. As they guided their
faithful burros up the path, Balaam felt that the
morning freshness would mitigate the pain his subject would feel at the mention of the word self-
denial. For the prophet knew how hard this dimen-

sion of the spiritual life was for one raised in the court of Moab. We can understand the enormity of his task, for he didn't have the supreme incentive to self-denial that the life and death of Jesus offers to each of us.

As Christians know, self-denial is founded on Jesus' words, "If a man wishes to come after me, he must deny his very self, take up his cross, and begin to follow in my footsteps" *(Matthew 16:24)*. This text is placed at a crucial point in Jesus' life. When he made it clear he had no intention of becoming a king, many left him. One day he asked his remaining disciples about his identity. After Peter replied, "You are the Messiah the Son of the living God," Jesus began to explain his coming death, and when Peter called him aside to straighten him out on the matter, he received a rebuke, "Get out of my sight, you satan! . . . You are not judging by God's standards but by man's" *(Matthew 16:23)*. Jesus could praise Peter's confession as inspired by the Father, but could only trace his rejection of the cross to weakness. He then turned to all *(cf. Mark 8:34)* and explained his doctrine of self-denial. Balaam was unknowingly practicing this doctrine by preferring fidelity to God's word to a high post in the Moabite court.

In rejecting the king's offer, Balaam was not allowing his life to be guided by human criteria, by weak flesh and blood, but by divine standards. And this is the essence of Christian self-denial: to reject or deny one's own norms and judgments when they are contrary to those of Christ. It is a refusal to

87

live independently of God. To deny one's self means to accept the Father's criteria, to judge as he does, and as a result of this, to take up the cross and follow Jesus.

Self-denial doesn't always mean doing what is contrary to our own desires. It means this sometimes, but not always. Balaam may have contracted such a dislike for the king of Moab that three burro loads of precious gems couldn't have kept him in Moab for more than a week. He was longing to get back to the banks of the Euphrates, so there was no need to act contrary to his desires by leaving. The essential thing in self-denial is to act as God's servant and to do what he wants, like it or not.

Scholars point to a deepening of Balaam's obedience to God's word. In the first oracle, he had merely repeated God's words (Numbers 23:12), but now his obedience is more active (v. 26). His judgment becomes more and more conformed to God's. This is what the Christian must do in imitation of Jesus (John 8:29). Self-denial then isn't always painful, for those who live on the summit of perfection spontaneously and joyfully do what God wants. This is the filial spirit Jesus brought: "The Son cannot do anything by himself — he can only do what he sees the Father doing. For whatever the Father does, the Son does likewise" (John 5:19). Self-denial means making oneself independent of whatever conditions us to think and judge contrary to or independently of the Father.

When the party reached the summit of Pisgah, they repeated the same rites of sacrifice and Balaam went to meet God. Balak felt that the last oracle may have failed because Balaam's view of the whole Israelite camp may have frightened him and thus inhibited the curse. Now by seeing only part of Israel, the curse should come freely. But all the king's efforts were in vain for Balaam inspired perhaps by another natural sign, such as a cloud in the shape of a bull or lion, pronounced a new blessing. God is holy and does not change and so will not retract his plans for Israel. The effects of his blessing of Israel will remain; Balaam can't change them, and no evil will come upon Israel. God is present in his people giving it the strength of a wild bull. He is its king and no power can harm it. Magic is useless for like a lion Israel will conquer its enemies. This power and presence of God are reenforced in the New Covenant by the presence and power of Christ.

The text describes, with some irony, how the king lowered his standard, at least momentarily: if you can't curse, at least don't bless. But in spite of two failures, Balak decided on a third try the next morning. And so the men began another descent and Balaam felt that after this humiliation the king would be better disposed to discuss the issue of mortification. For his majesty, this oracle was what Christians call a cross: something painful or troublesome. Self-denial isn't always painful, but the cross is. It means fatigue, sorrow, daily problems and anything that hurts. But the cross can be distinguished from another form of suffering which Christian spirituality calls "the passion." Jesus suffered at Nazareth. This was a cross but it isn't usually considered a part of his passion. This word is reserved for suffering that is humanly inexplicable, for pure suffering which has no apparent reason or good effect. The suffering caused by work and ordinary living is easy to justify, but suffering that shows no immediate advantage or purpose is hard to understand. Things like sickness, old age, failure and abandonment by others add a new dimension to suffering. The suffering of children and the innocent is a particular stumbling block. But Christ brings meaning even to this. By accepting his passion, his cup of pure suffering, he manifests its redemptive and sanctifying value. This doctrine would have consoled even the frustrated king of Moab.

Since he lived before the coming of Christ, Balaam couldn't realize the value of pure suffering but he could see that Balak was inflicting unnecessary pain on himself by resisting God's will. Like a good director, he tried to explain this to the king. Today the director must insist on the importance of the cross. This doesn't mean he should push his subjects to idealize suffering and constantly seek it, for this would be an unhealthy attitude, since life is a mixture of joy and pain. But since no Christian life will be without purifications and daily crosses, the subject must be ready for them and not be discouraged when they come.

In St. Paul's mind, Christ's passion and resurrection are a single undivided reality, like two sides of a coin. And although Christian life is a participation in Christ's resurrection, it continues to share his suffering. The apostle has a luminous passage on this: "I wish to know Christ and the power flowing from his resurrection; likewise to know how to share in his sufferings..." *(Philippians 3:10).* This is the chronological order his own experience of Christ had followed and it marks the ordinary way for the Christian: a knowledge of the risen Christ and then an introduction to his sufferings. The participation in the resurrection at baptism should inspire a desire to share in Christ's sufferings not only sacramentally, but actually. Thus Christian life is lived between two resurrections — one baptismal, the other eschatological. It is a race that occurs between two resurrections: "...but I am racing to grasp the prize if possible, since I have been grasped by Christ" *(Philippians 3:12).* This doctrine would not only have consoled Balaam but another great counsellor, Job, whom suffering forced to move his counsel seat from the city gate to a dunghill outside.

Balak could only see one meaning in suffering: it was an evil and inflicted by the gods as a punishment. Chemosh was mad at his people and was delivering them into the hands of Israel. An inscription written about 830 B.C. by Mesha, king of Moab, gives this as the reason for Israel's victory over Moab. "As for Omri, King of Israel, he humbled Moab many years for Chemosh was angry at his land." At times a director may find remnants of this false idea among his subjects and he must remind them that neither Jesus nor his mother were sinners. In God's plan, suffering isn't a punishment but a sign of God's special love. As Paul says, "... for it is your special privilege to take Christ's part — not only to believe in him but also to suffer for him" *(Philippians 1:29).*

One delicate aspect of moritification that Balaam had to bring up was the voluntary type. Balak was acquainted with fasting, for example, since the Moabites fasted just as the Assyrians did *(Jonah 3:5).* But as with other religious practices, the king had a mechanical attitude toward it and thought it influenced the gods automatically. But the evangelical concept of penance is quite different. Penance here is a voluntary corporal affliction undertaken as a participation in the passion of Christ. One of its most common forms is fasting. Jesus fasted *(Matthew 4:2)* to set an example and predicted that his disciples would too after his passion "when the groom is taken away" *(Matthew 9:15).* Fasting, of course, is not the only form of voluntary affliction, although it was a popular one from the beginning of Christianity. Some early monks carried it to excess and made it the whole of the spiritual life. They fasted furiously and had fasting contests. The main reason was that fasting can be measured, while interior growth in union with God can't. Even though the latter is more difficult than the former, the monks wanted to do something for God that was visible and tangible. Since no ascetic practice is easier to measure than this, it became the royal road to heaven for thousands of simple and unlettered monks who lovingly starved for Christ.

Like any good director, Balaam wanted to leave his subject some guiding principles in this matter of voluntary mortification. He knew it was important because he had learned that when a subject began to lose interest in spiritual growth the first thing he dropped was penance. He knew too that it couldn't be forced on people for this is like making them eat undigestible food. He therefore dropped a suggestion to the king that after a life of unbridled passion, it is often helpful to undertake some serious mortification.

But as the prophet anticipated, the royal mind was simply closed on this point. It would be a waste of time to tell Balak that mortification must be centered on purifying disordered affections and passions; first, in so far as these lead to sin, and then in so far as they cause infidelity to our present graces and duties. Furthermore, both interior and exterior senses must be purified, i.e. restrained from anything contrary to Christian temperance. This voluntary penance must cover not only evil things, but good ones when God clearly asks us to sacrifice them for a greater good, because a spiritual man never weighs good against evil, but good against a greater good. This mortification must not encroach upon our duties nor must it always be restricted to fulfilling them. Its forms and intensity depend on God's call to each. A director should help the subject heed that call.

The principle that the greater the suffering, the greater the number of souls saved is not exact, for what saves souls is suffering from a motive of love. There is no more salvific value in suffering from self-will than in having a good time from self-will. The subject should be warned not to impose anything on himself that he can't carry out gracefully. If a particular practice depresses, causes temptations or just plain horror, it would be better to wait until more spiritual endurance is achieved. A director must not drive a subject up the mountain of mortification, for the impulse should come from within. He must not impose his own views but help the individual to do spontaneously what he feels God is calling him to do. Balak didn't seem to feel that Chemosh cared what he did along this line as long as he showed up for the sacrifices.

Balaam's final remark certainly pleased the king because he told him that a spirit of peace and serenity should dominate the spiritual life, and that mortification must never become its center.

8

The Third Oracle: Formation in Fraternal Love

Balak said to Balaam, 'Come then, let me take you somewhere else. From there perhaps it will please God to curse them.' So Balak led Balaam to the summit of Peor, dominating the desert. Then Balaam said to Balak, 'Build me seven altars here and find me seven bulls and seven rams.' Balak did as Balaam asked, and offered a holocaust of one bull and one ram on each altar.

Balaam then saw that it pleased Yahweh to bless Israel. He did not go as before to seek omens but turned towards the wilderness. Raising his eyes Balaam saw Israel, encamped by tribes; the spirit of God came on him and he declaimed his poem. He said:

'The oracle of Balaam son of Beor,
the oracle of the man with far-seeing eyes,
the oracle of one who hears the word of
    God.
He sees what Shaddai makes him see,

receives the divine answer, and his eyes are
   opened.
How fair are your tents, O Jacob!
How fair your dwellings, Israel!
Like valleys that stretch afar,
like gardens by the banks of a river,
like aloes planted by Yahweh,
like cedars beside the waters!
A hero arises from their stock,
he reigns over countless peoples.
His king is greater than Agag,
his majesty is exalted.
God brings him out of Egypt,
he is like the wild ox's horns to him.
He feeds on the carcase of his enemies,
and breaks their bones in pieces.
He has crouched, he has lain down,
like a lion, like a lioness;
who dare rouse him?
Blessed be those who bless you,
and accursed be those who curse you!'

Balak flew into a rage with Balaam. He beat
his hands together and said to Balaam, 'I
brought you to curse my enemies, and you bless
them three times over! Be off with you, and go
home. I promised to load you with honours.
Yahweh himself has deprived you of them.'
Balaam answered Balak, 'Did I not tell the
messengers you sent me: Even if Balak gave me
his house full of gold and silver I could not go
against the order of Yahweh and do anything of
my own accord, good or evil; what Yahweh says
is what I will say. . . .'

Numbers 23:27-24:13

Since Baal-Peor, the third mountain selected
by Balak, was only separated from Nebo by a

ravine, the party passed the night in tents and began the ascent early in the day. Balaam knew this might be his last chance with the king, so he began to speak about his relations with other men. But how could he explain fraternal love to a Moabite who looked at others through the eyes of Cain? He didn't have the perfect example of interpersonal relationships Jesus left in the Parable of the Good Samaritan. He had to follow a different road.

The prophet told his majesty that he was viewing other men, especially the Israelites, as objects. He regarded them as something fully comprehensible, completed, numerable, quantifiable, completely exposed, and indifferent. But no man can be reduced to a series of data for a questionnaire, for there is always more to him than can be understood. Neither is another man something final and complete from which no surprises are to be expected, since human existence is a creation of new possibilities, not a mere development of what is already possessed. And rather than a numerable reality, man is a nameable one, called into existence by name by his creator *(Genesis 17:5; Isaiah 45:3-4)*. Every man then is a *hapax legomenon,* a word that God pronounces only once. Man as a person, then, isn't quantitatively comparable to other men but qualitatively incomparable. Objects can be compared but persons as such cannot be unless they are objectified.

The prophet told Balak that while an object is completely exposed, is patent (so that to see what

97

is on its backside, we only need to shift our perspective by walking behind it), man is not wholly visible — he is latent; there is always something in him we can't see no matter how many different angles we view him from. He then suggested that in the king's frantic race from mountain to mountain, to view Israel from different perspectives, he was nursing a concept of men as objects. And if Israel was an object, its disappearance was something to which he was indifferent. When we lose a person we love, it leaves a scar in us; when we lose someone we regard as an object, we remain indifferent.

Balaam explained to the Moabite that he was also regarding Israel as an obstacle, something thrown in his path. This can happen physically, when someone pushes in front of us in line, for example; or it can happen in a more invisible way, when someone gets the promotion we had been hoping for and so blocks our way up the ladder. Israel embodied both types of obstacle for Balak. He had his own plans for the pasture land they were camped on and so they were a visible obstacle. In addition this checked his aspirations to become a business tycoon in the region by shipping mutton to Mesopotamia and so they were an invisible obstacle.

Balak didn't realize that if others were an obstacle to him, it was because they resisted him; but without this resistance no man can develop. As birds can't fly without the air that resists their wings, so no man can grow without the resistance offered by others. Without obstacles, i.e. persons, institutions, customs, etc. to resist him, man would be an empty reality, lacking content. Balaam therefore tried to suggest that Balak's meeting with Israel didn't have to be impoverishing; it could become an enrichment for both of them. They could go into the shipping business together and double their profits.

But Balak treated Israel as an obstacle. There are three ways of eliminating another when he is regarded as an obstacle. The first and simplest, the one the king had chosen, is physical assassination. The long-desired curse was only the first step in this process. Once it had weakened Israel, the Moabite army would appear to administer the coup de grace. Today physical assassination is rarely resorted to by those engaged in the spiritual life so we need examine it no further.

The second way of eliminating human obstacles, however, is always a possibility among mature Christians: personal assassination. It consists in leaving the individual's physical being intact but hindering the full development of his personal life, his possibilities and his talents. In modern politics, for example, an adversary is often reduced to silence by making it impossible for him to defend himself or express his opinions. The same thing can happen in religious circles where those who don't share the proper theological or spiritual opinions are quietly assassinated. This form would not appeal to Balak, however, because it would be too slow.

The third manner of disposing of someone we regard as an obstacle is to avoid him, to treat him as if he didn't exist or as if he isn't to be taken seriously. This can be licit and even necessary in some cases. No one should be ashamed to avoid someone who has signed a contract to kill him, for example. But outside of such cases, this is the most dissimulated and subtle form of eliminating another person. The priest and the Levite used it when they noticed the wounded man on the Jericho road. They acted as if he didn't exist, and if they had been asked when they arrived at Jericho whether they had seen a wounded man on the road, they would have replied, "I saw no one." This kind of assassination can be practiced by turning one's eyes away from another, by avoiding his name when it would be charitable just to mention it, etc. Since this can also be the cruelest form of annihilation, it might have tempted Balak if he hadn't already set his heart on the first form.

Balaam warned the king that if the other man responded in kind to an assassination attempt, a war would result. Whoever wins makes the other his servant, or at least imposes some pact on him that eliminates him as far as possible. Long after Balak's death, King David conquered Moab and made its people his instruments, i.e. objects for the realization of his own ends. By subjecting Moab to tribute, it became an instrument for Israel's enrichment. This is the most common way of treating others as objects. It means saying implicitly that since I can, I have decided to use you as an object for my own ends; your possibilities will no longer be yours but mine. The two extreme forms of this instrumentalizing of another are slavery and prostitution, but there are many less intense forms.

These ideas that Balaam dropped as seeds into the king's heart didn't have the motivating power of the Parable of the Good Samaritan. In telling this story, Jesus, the "Wonder-Counsellor" *(Isaiah 9:5)* upon whom "a spirit of wisdom and understanding, a spirit of counsel and of strength" *(Isaiah 11:2)* has rested, tries to teach his disciples to resolve all problems in the light of love rather than of law. The Jewish doctor who asks Jesus, "And who is my neighbor?" *(Luke 10:29)* is a jurist looking for the conditions needed to apply a precept. He wants to know in which precise cases he is obliged to love another as his neighbor. His attitude is caustic. Jesus' story tells him he must listen to the law of the heart in solving these cases rather than to legal prescriptions. The question with which the story ends: "Which of these three, in your opinion, was neighbor to the man who fell in with the robbers?" *(Luke 10:36)* intentionally inverts the terms of the questions that precedes the story. Instead of "Who is my neighbor?" it becomes "To whom am I a neighbor?" thereby shifting the center from the "I" to the "thou." But since Jesus, who bent over a wounded humanity and saved it after it fell among robber demons had not yet come, Balaam had to do his best to help the king without this teaching.

No matter which mountain Balak viewed

Israel from it looked bad to him because all he saw was its human dimension, while it always looked good to Balaam since he always saw its divine dimension. Balak is like those inside and outside the Church today who can only see the sins of its members. It is true that the Church has at times manifested real poverty of vision, has been short-sighted in its planning, has forgotten the poor and allied itself with the rich, has followed the times rather than creatively gone in advance of them and has opposed scientific progress rather than support it. But these and other deficiencies in the Church are only one side of it. Meditation on them must be balanced by the thought that in spite of its failings the Church has brought man the possibility of a personal encounter with Christ. Thanks to the Church, man can become a contemporary of Christ by participating in his Eucharist and by listening to his word. Buddha, Socrates or any other human personality will always remain distant and foreign; through the voice of the Church, the living voice of Christ reaches us and daily inter-prellates us. This benefit alone outweighs by far all the mistakes accumulated during its two-thousand-year history. One of the permanent fruits of spiritual direction should be a love of the Church and a desire to serve it in the role for which God has equipped us.

Balaam didn't succeed in leading Balak to a love of Israel and the modern director will meet Christians who talk about the Church as if they were outside it. This lack of love for the Church on the part of many of its members is a major ingredient in the present crisis. They criticize it as if they weren't a part of it. They objectify it, just as Balak turned Israel into an object. Instead of being part of them, it is exterior to them.

Balak's blindness to Israel's value must not be judged too harshly, however, because the most important aspects of the people of God are not always the most evident. Without faith, the Church's inner mystery can't be detected. Its reference to Christ and to the Gospel is its essential core. It is also a holy community, a communion of saints in possession of sacred things. But most people only see an exterior organization or rites, laws and traditions. The director must insist that the Church isn't something exterior to man's spiritual development but the source of pure and authentic spirituality. For the spirituality that Christ brought is engendered, strengthened and perfected within and by the Church. Like St. Augustine, the director must constantly remind his subject, "Live united to this Mother who has engendered you."

Every member of the Church must live one aspect of its mystery in an exemplary way. He should feel that in the heart of the Church and in the midst of the world he is love or adoration, evangelical word or thought, presence to the poor or distance for the sake of prayer, a source of scandal to illuminate the dark spots of human life and sinfulness, or a source of consolation to alleviate its sorrows and despair. But no one within the Church should look on it as a spectator from without as Balak did.

There are many ways of building up the Church today, but normally the director, like Balaam, should merely point out the possibilities to his subject. He should tell him the Church needs prayer and contemplation, missionary work and service in hospitals and on the streets, but leave him free to decide which direction his work is going to take. While watching to be sure that the subject's dispositions are correct in making his choice, he won't make it for him.

If a subject decides that his role is something completely unheard of or novel, the director shouldn't try to exclude it but see if the signs of a prudent choice are present, for God likes to spring surprises on his people. Of course if a subject like Balak were to decide to do something far exceeding his possibilities — to imitate Suppiluliumas I, for example — the director may conclude that he is suffering from a delusion and help him make a new decision. The essential thing is to help the subject find his own charism, ordinary or extraordinary.

With so many changes in the world today, there is a strong temptation to try to fit into an imaginary community instead of into the real one at hand. A director will insist on the possibilities that are open to the subject and not allow him to waste time with pipe dreams. Balaam's whole intention was to help Balak integrate himself into the new situation taking shape around him without attempting to escape. No one is in the world just to save his own soul. Each has a contribution to make and must find it and make it realistically. St. Therese of Lisieux's example is stimulating. When she had hardly reached adulthood, she could already write, "In the heart of my mother the Church, I will be love."

The royal party now reached the summit of Baal-Peor and Balak repeated the altar work and sacrifices. Balaam didn't bother with an omen this time but was immediately filled with the Spirit, which gives more solemnity to the oracle that follows. This poem is very close in literary form, style and theme to Jacob's blessing *(Genesis 49)*. The prophet first mentioned his perfect open eye ready to see God's visions and hear his words. His vision was of Israel camped below him like an immense green garden with magnificent trees watered by a stream. This paradisiacal image refers to Israel's material prosperity but also expresses the spiritual nature of this well-being. It is a popular biblical image of spiritual renewal *(Psalm 1:3; Jeremiah 17:7 f; Ezekiel 47:1-12)*.

Balaam next described the reasons for Israel's prosperity: first, its demographic fecundity, "its seed in abundant waters," as the Hebrew text in verse 7a may be translated; secondly, its king (v. 7b); and finally the God who led it out of Egypt and continues to protect it (v. 8). The question, "Who will arouse him?" is a challenge. Israel's present prosperity is definitive and a pledge for the future. Just as his divination skill allowed Balaam to predict the future by interpreting natural signs, so the Spirit now inspired him to predict a glorious future for Israel by contemplating its present condition. The reference to the king of course was inserted by the Yahwist authors who preserved this oracle.

This was too much for Balak. In spite of his sacred duty of hospitality, he burst into anger and ordered his guest out of the kingdom. The king made it clear that no reward would come his way; Balaam would never be installed as spiritual director to the court of Moab. The king also thought that God himself would not reward the prophet, since he hadn't fulfilled his duty by refusing to curse when that is what he was hired for. Balaam humbly reminded him that he promised no curse and was indifferent to rewards. But then, faced with the king's hardened heart, he warned him that hard times were in store for Moab. This introduces the final oracle that will terminate this directional relationship.

9

The Fourth Oracle:
Direction's Fundamental Form
Love of Christ

"But now that I am about to go to my own
people, let me first warn you what this people
will do to your people in the days to come."
Then Balaam gave voice to his oracle:

The utterance of Balaam, son of Beor,
  the utterance of the man whose eye
    is true,
The utterance of one who hears what God
    says,
  and knows what the Most High knows,
Of one who sees what the Almighty sees,
  enraptured and with eyes unveiled.
I see him, though not now;
  I behold him, though not near:
A star shall advance from Jacob,
  and a staff shall rise from Israel,
That shall smite the brows of Moab,
  and the skulls of all the Shuthites,
Till Edom is dispossessed,
  and no fugitive is left in Seir.

Israel shall do valiantly,
  and Jacob shall overcome his foes.

Upon seeing Amalek, Balam gave voice to his oracle:

First of the peoples was Amalek,
  but this end is to perish forever.

Upon seeing the Kenites, he gave voice to his oracle:

Your abode is enduring, O smith,
  and your nest is set on a cliff;
Yet destined for burning —
  even as I watch — are your inhabitants.

Upon seeing . . . he gave voice to his oracle:

Alas, who shall survive of Ishmael,
  to deliver his people from the hands of
    the Kittim?
When they have conquered Asshur and
    conquered Eber,
  He too shall perish forever.

The Babylonians were great astrologers and at times interpreted wandering stars as omens of Habiru raids. The Habiru seem to have been nomads or semi-nomads who often raided settlements during the second millennium. One text reads: "If a wandering star appears at the beginning of Kisilimmu, there will be Habiru, there will be a defeat." The parallel with verse 17 of our oracle is obvious: "(If) a star shall advance from Jacob, a staff shall rise from Israel." A star may have furnished the omen for this poem. But whatever the precise wording Balaam used, the Yahwists have adapted his oracle to their own situation in David's time. For it is now a victory song for King David. The first two oracles referred only to the people, the third made a passing reference to the king, but this one is centered on him. It contains both blessings and curses and describes Israel's situation at the beginning of the Davidic monarchy: the conquest is over and a new era of hope and prosperity has begun. Yet this oracle is a real prophecy, because the present conditions it mentions are seen continuing into the future. Not only David but all his descendants will be victorious over their enemies. All Christian commentators see a prophecy of Christ here; the Venerable Bede says the star is the Church or Mary, from whom Christ the light comes forth.

This oracle on the star of Jacob gives the tone and foundation for all spiritual direction: the love of Christ. A director isn't primarily interested in producing perfect men, but men completely dedicated to Christ. He wants to form disciples of Christ. Throughout the slow directional process, Christ should be presented at the heart of the Trinity as the Father's revelation through the Spirit that pours love into our hearts so that through love of him and of those with whom he entered into solidarity we can return to the Father. This love of Christ with its essential fraternal dimension is the whole point of the spiritual project one undertakes by seeking direction. It is another way of saying that charity is the essence of perfection, a charity that has become a passionate love for Christ.

St. Paul is a man in love with Christ. He sees

the essential Christian attitudes as consequences of one's love for Christ *(Philippians 2:5)*. Christian patience, for example, can never mean simply not getting impatient, but must reflect and participate in Christ's patience. Balaam's patient attitude toward the king of Moab was a foreshadowing of that of Christ.

This centering on Christ should also extend to the subject's attitudes toward his sins and failings. They won't bother him because they hurt his pride or make him feel his weakness, but because they offend God and are infidelities to Christ. By helping him feel his nothingness, they open his heart more to Christ. Balak gave no indication that his faults caused him any pain, rather those around him felt the pain.

This theme should not only form direction's atmosphere but should be treated directly. A good way to do this is to devote an interview now and then to explaining a passage of the Gospel, helping the subject to penetrate Jesus' attitudes and to find applications to his own life. Thus friendship with the risen Christ will gradually become the main support of this Christian's life, a support Balaam never had.

The second part of this oracle contains some menacing words about Moab and Edom (v. 17b-19), and then, finally, three small oracles against the Amalekites, the Kenites and an unidentified people close the interview between the two men. These last three oracles (v. 20-24) are cast in a literary form that was developed later by the

110

prophets and was called "oracles against the nations." They haven't been integrated into the Balaam story like the other four, but are simply tacked on. Scholars think they existed before the story was first put into writing and were retained to fill out the sacred number seven for Balaam's oracles as well as to amplify the list of David's victories. The Amalekites were an ancient Arab tribe which lived south of the Negeb and was always hostile to Israel. Both Saul and David defeated them. The Kenites lived south of the Dead Sea. Some scholars think the third people, like the first two, must have been southerners. Since all three fought against Israel and were defeated by David, they fittingly close the list of his victories. Today they teach us that God is defending his chosen people and that all its enemies' efforts are in vain. The Fathers read them as messianic and eschatological messages containing not only words about the past but promises for the present and future. God will defend his people until the end of time. The Christian will replace their Old Testament tone with Christ's attitude toward his enemies. He will be willing to suffer and pray for their conversion rather than rejoice over their defeat.

10

The Parting of the Ways

For the first time, Balak was left speechless. He simply climbed on his burro and returned home in silence. Balaam did the same for as St. Augustine remarks, the burro's gift of speech was only temporary and the good animal didn't go on talking to its master for the rest of its life. As he rode along, the prophet reflected on his recent experience. He had to admit that he had failed. A director's work is hard, monotonous and often thankless. At the same time it is so complex and sublime that he keenly feels the danger of making mistakes. The thanklessness and danger combine to make it a heavy load for any man's back.

Balaam knew that he was expected to adapt the spiritual tradition he had received to each of his subjects. He knew this was a hard drawn-out task for which there were no shortcuts. He didn't go to Balak with a panacea for his problems. He was too wise to oversimplify the spiritual life for there are two kinds of simplicity: one proper to children at life's beginning, and another for the mature. Children are simple because they haven't met life's major problems; mature persons are simple when they have learned to meet and solve these problems. But it would be ridiculous to try to hand a child a simplicity attained after hard years of experience, for no matter how much one wants to spare the child the anguish of the maturation process, it can't be done. No oversimplified spiritual secret can save man from the spiritual growing-up process. This was a consoling thought for Balaam and he reflected that no matter how many high-priced directors the king imported, he wasn't going to mature without making the same effort as everyone else.

Balaam didn't have to accuse himself of applying the same spiritual formula to all his clients either. The director who does this is like the physician who hands out the same medicine to all his patients. God hasn't endowed any elements in this world with such virtues that any one of them will cure everything from baldness and snakebite to cancer. The director should not search for spiritual cure-alls for his task is to diagnose needs and apply the correct remedy to each. Authentic direction is always individual because of the individual differences in men and women and because of the unique and unrepeatable imprint of the Spirit on each.

Balaam was aware that some directors in the

Near East would have told the king to simply follow the motions of the Spirit. But the prophet knew that the Moabite was still too immature to take this path. In order to teach the king how to solve his own problems and make his own decisions, he would have told him to report afterwards on the decisions he made and to talk them over. He would have learned gradually to walk by himself and in the right way. The director who wants subjects to follow orders rather than to choose their own path is putting himself in the Spirit's place.

Even if Balak had asked for concrete decisions in the first steps of his spiritual life, Balaam would have told him, "I think your dispositions are good enough for you to make this decision for yourself." And if those dispositions were faulty, he would have helped the king improve them. But it was too late now. Balak had turned him out. After all his efforts at helping him produce a harvest, he proved to be a dry field.

Balaam knew that there are cases when both the director and subject feel they are getting nowhere, but that the director must not lose confidence in his subject or in the Spirit. He was aware too that some plants only bear fruit after years of care. He had an aversion for directors who only had time for privileged souls and who insisted they bear instant fruit. His own lot had rather meant sweating it out with tough cases hoping for whatever fruit God might give. And often the subject had the same attitude toward him, doubting his competence and wondering when the ecstasies were going to start. But the prophet had met cases as hard as Balak's before and knew that magnanimity was the only solution. "Trust 'til I bust," he kept repeating to himself on these occasions.

Another reason for his wariness was the fear of making a mistake. He might ruin someone spiritually. One of his own spiritual masters had told him that this feeling was a good sign since the director who didn't think he could slip up was sure to hand out the wrong medicine. He told him too that there wasn't a counsellor in the entire Near East who hadn't made mistakes, and three of his own spiritual sons had hung themselves as a result of his guidance. But what surgeon can perform a delicate operation without danger of killing the patient? The director must, after prayer and thought, make the judgments he has decided are correct and then trust that God won't let the subject suffer from them. If he avoids speaking *ex cathedra,* as if the Spirit had appointed him as spokesman for this region, and remains humbly dependent on that Spirit, he will have done what he could and must go ahead without expecting miraculous signs to confirm his decisions. And if he later finds that his counsel was wrong, he should correct it if he can and if he can't, then he will have learned a lesson for the future and should not give up trying to help weak and sinful men like himself on their road to God.

After describing the anguish a director feels

when he realizes that one of his subjects is spiritually dead, St. John of Avila writes, "Therefore, whoever wants to be a father should have a tender and very fleshy heart in order to have compassion on his sons, which in itself is a great martyrdom; and another heart of iron to endure the blows that their death causes so they won't demolish the father, or make him abandon his office, or become depressed, or pass days doing nothing but weep." St. John says weeping is a luxury the director can't afford because while he mopes over the death of one subject, he puts the others in danger. If his sons are good, he has to give them "very careful care," and if they are bad, they cause him "very sad sadness." So the director feels constant misgivings, and must always be on guard and ever at prayer, for he has made his own life depend on theirs as St. Paul says: "For now we live, if you stand fast in the Lord" *(1 Thessalonians 3:8)*. This is certainly an echo of Balaam's experiences.

After writing this and some other counsel to a director, St. John goes on to say that this advice "is only drawn from the experience of the mistakes that I have made; I wish that my having erred could mean that no one else would, and if this were so I would regard my mistakes as well employed." This would have consoled the prophet as he rode home wondering if he had followed the right road in approaching his royal subject.

So far no archaeologist's spade has turned up any of Balaam's spiritual letters. But it is possible that after leaving the prophet God's words may have begun to work on the king and bring about a conversion. If Balak decided then that Balaam was the only director he could speak to freely, and if God refused to let the prophet go back to Moab, spiritual letters may have passed by burro from the Euphrates to the Moabite court. Normally direction should be given orally, and when the director moves the subject should look up a new one rather than live from the mailbox. By the time a letter arrives, the subject's state may have changed and made the advice useless or even harmful. The written word is also easy to misinterpret. But since the prophet already knew the king well, he may have accepted this task. We can be sure his letters were short and full of concrete advice and that they contained nothing that would cause embarrassment or harm if they fell into the hands of a third party.

When Balaam finally reached his home on the right bank of the Euphrates and put his faithful burro out to pasture and his bag of omens on the shelf, he went into his oratory and silently offered a prayer to the God who had guided him on his journey and begged him to direct Balak, king of Moab and son of Cain, into the path of love.

LINGER WITH ME
Moments Aside With Jesus 2.95

Rev. Msgr. David E. Rosage. God is calling us to a listening posture in prayer in the desire to experience him at the very core of our being. Monsignor Rosage helps us to "come by ourselves apart" daily and listen to what Jesus is telling us in Scripture.

PRAYING WITH SCRIPTURE IN THE HOLY LAND:
Daily Meditations With the Risen Jesus 2.45

Msgr. David E. Rosage. Herein is offered a daily meeting with the Risen Jesus in those Holy Places which He sanctified by His human presence. Three hundred and sixty-five scripture texts are selected and blended with the pilgrimage experiences of the author, a retreat master, and well-known writer on prayer.

DISCOVERING PATHWAYS TO PRAYER 1.95

Msgr. David E. Rosage. Following Jesus was never meant to be dull, or worse, just duty-filled. Those who would aspire to a life of prayer and those who have already begun, will find this book amazingly thorough in its scripture-punctuated approach.

"A simple but profound book which explains the many ways and forms of prayer by which the person hungering for closer union with God may find him." **Emmanuel Spillane, O.C.S.O., Abbot, Our Lady of the Holy Trinity Abbey, Huntsville, Utah.**

Order from your bookstore or
LIVING FLAME PRESS, Locust Valley, N.Y. 11560

REASONS FOR REJOICING
Experiences in Christian Hope   1.75

Rev. Kenneth J. Zanca. The author asks: "Do we really or rarely have a sense of excitement, mystery, and wonder in the presence of God?" His book offers a path to rejuvenation in Christian faith, hope, and love. It deals with prayer, forgiveness, worship and other religious experiences in a learned and penetrating, yet simple, non-technical manner. **Religion Teachers' Journal.**

"It is a refreshing Christian approach to the Good News, always emphasizing the love and mercy of God in our lives, and our response to that love in Christian hope." **Brother Patrick Hart, Secretary to the late Thomas Merton.**

MARY:
Pathway to Fruitfulness   1.95

John Randall, STD., Helen P. Hawkinson, Sharyn Malloy. Mary is shown to be an exemplar of fruitful Christian living in her role as model relative, suffering servant and seat of wisdom. Her growing role as mediator between Catholics and Protestants is also highlighted.

FORMED BY HIS WORD:
Scriptural Patterns of Prayer   1.95

Rev. Malcolm Cornwell, C.P. Father Cornwell opens the wealth of Luke's teachings on prayer for individuals, teachers and prayer groups. Recommended for liturgy committees, priests and all who are interested in family or group prayer based on the scriptures and the liturgy of the hours. **National Bulletin on Liturgy, Canada.**

JONAH:
Spirituality of a Runaway Prophet 1.75

Roman Ginn, o.c.s.o. While acquiring a new appreciation for this very human prophet, we come to see that his story is really our own. It reveals a God whose love is unwavering yet demanding, for if we are to experience the freedom of mature Christians, we must enter the darkness of the tomb with Christ, as Jonah did, in order to rise to new life.

POOR IN SPIRIT:
Awaiting All From God 1.75

Cardinal Garrone. Not a biography of the Mother Teresa of her age, this spiritual account of Jeanne Jugan's complete and joyful abandonment to God leads us to a vibrant understanding of spiritual and material poverty.

DESERT SILENCE:
A Way of Prayer for an Unquiet Age 1.75

Rev. Alan J. Placa. The pioneering efforts of the men and women of the early church who went out into the desert to find union with the Lord has relevance for those of us today who are seeking the pure uncluttered desert place within to have it filled with the loving silence of God's presence.

THE LOVE EXPLOSION:
Human Experience and the Christian Mystery 2.50

Rev. Robert E. Lauder. Man's search for meaning is explored as is the nature of "personhood" and the mystery of love as it applies to relationships among persons. Secularism is regarded as a challenge, not a threat.

THE BOOK OF REVELATION:
What Does It Really Say?   1.95

Rev. John Randall, S.T.D. The most discussed book of the Bible today is examined by a scripture expert in relation to much that has been published on the Truth. A simply written and revealing presentation.

. . . AND I WILL FILL THIS HOUSE WITH GLORY:
Renewal Within a Suburban Parish   1.50

Rev. James A. Brassil. This book helps answer the questions: What is the Charismatic Renewal doing for the Church as a whole? and What is the prayer group doing for the parish? With a vibrant prayer life and a profound devotion to the Eucharist, this Long Island prayer group has successfully endured the growing pains inherent to the spiritual life, the fruit of which is offered to the reader.

CONTEMPLATIVE PRAYER:
Problems and an Approach
for the Ordinary Christian   1.75

Rev. Alan J. Placa. This inspiring book covers much ground: the struggle of prayer, growth in familiarity with the Lord and the sharing process. In addition, he clearly outlines a method of contemplative prayer for small groups based on the belief that private communion with God is essential to, and must precede, shared prayer. The last chapter provides model prayers, taken from our Western heritage, for the enrichment of private prayer experience.

Order from your bookstore or
LIVING FLAME PRESS, Locust Valley, N.Y. 11560

THE ONE WHO LISTENS:
A Book of Prayer   2.25

Rev. Michael Hollings and Etta Gullick. Here the Spirit speaks through men and women of the past (St. John of the Cross, Thomas More, Dietrich Bonhoeffer), and present (Michel Quoist, Mother Teresa, Malcolm Boyd). There are also prayers from men of other faiths such as Muhammed and Tagore. God meets us where we are and since men share in sorrow, joy and anxiety, *their* prayers are *our* prayers. This is a book that will be outworn, perhaps, but never outgrown.

ENFOLDED BY CHRIST:
An Encouragement to Pray   1.95

Rev. Michael Hollings. This book helps us toward giving our lives to God in prayer yet at the same time remaining totally available to our fellowman — a difficult but possible feat. Father's sharing of his own difficulties and his personal approach convince us that "if he can do it, we can." We find in the author a true spiritual guardian and friend.

SOURCE OF LIFE:
The Eucharist and Christian Living   1.50

Rev. Rene Voillaume. A powerful testimony to the vital part the Eucharist plays in the life of a Christian. It is a product of a man for whom Christ in the Eucharist is nothing less than all.

Order from your bookstore or
LIVING FLAME PRESS, Locust Valley, N.Y. 11560

SEEKING PURITY OF HEART:
The Gift of Ourselves to God
illus. 1.50

Joseph Breault. For those of us who feel that we do not live up to God's calling, that we have sin of whatever shade within our hearts. This book shows how we can begin a journey which will lead from our personal darkness to wholeness in Christ's light — a purity of heart. Clear, practical help is given us in the constant struggle to free ourselves from the deceptions that sin has planted along all avenues of our lives.

Order from your bookstore or
LIVING FLAME PRESS, Locust Valley, N.Y. 11560

Books by Venard Polusney, O. Carm.

UNION WITH THE LORD IN PRAYER
Beyond Meditation to Affective Prayer Aspiration and Contemplation   1.00

"A magnificent piece of work. It touches on all the essential points of Contemplative Prayer. Yet it brings such a sublime subject down to the level of comprehension of the 'man in the street,' and in such an encouraging way."
Abbott James Fox, O.C.S.O. (former superior of Thomas Merton at the Abbey of Gethsemani)

ATTAINING SPIRITUAL MATURITY FOR CON-TEMPLATION
(According to St. John of the Cross)   1.00

"I heartily recommend this work with great joy that at last the sublime teachings of St. John of the Cross have been brought down to the understanding of the ordinary Christian without at the same time watering them down. For all (particularly for charismatic Christians) hungry for greater contemplation."
Rev. George A. Maloney, S.J., Editor of Diakonia, Professor of Patristics and Spirituality, Fordham University.

THE PRAYER OF LOVE . . .
The Art of Aspiration   1.95

"It is the best book I have read which evokes the simple and loving response to remain in love with the Lover. To read it meditatively, to imbibe its message of love, is to have it touch your life and become part of what you are."
Mother Dorothy Guilbuilt, O. Carm., Superior General, Lacombe, La.

Order from your bookstore or
LIVING FLAME PRESS, Locust Valley, N.Y. 11560

LIVING FLAME PRESS
BOX 74, LOCUST VALLEY, N.Y. 11560

Quantity

_____	**Linger With Me — 2.95**
_____	**Mary: Pathway to Fruitfulness — 1.95**
_____	**The Judas Within — 1.95**
_____	**Formed by His Word — 1.95**
_____	**Jonah — 1.75**
_____	**Poor in Spirit — 1.75**
_____	**Desert Silence — 1.75**
_____	**Praying With Scripture in the Holy Land — 2.45**
_____	**Discovering Pathways to Prayer — 1.95**
_____	**Reasons for Rejoicing — 1.75**
_____	**Contemplative Prayer — 1.75**
_____	**The One Who Listens — 2.25**
_____	**Enfolded by Christ — 1.95**
_____	**Source of Life — 1.50**
_____	**Seeking Purity of Heart — 1.50**
_____	**The Love Explosion — 2.50**
_____	**The Book of Revelation — 1.95**
_____	**And I Will Fill This House With Glory — 1.50**
_____	**Union With the Lord in Prayer — 1.00**
_____	**Attaining Spiritual Maturity — 1.00**
_____	**The Prayer of Love — 1.95**

QUANTITY ORDER: DISCOUNT RATES

For convents, prayer groups, etc.: $10 to $25 = 10%;
$26 to $50 = 15%; over $50 = 20%. Booksellers: 40%; 30 days net.

NAME _____

ADDRESS _____

CITY_____ STATE_____ ZIP_____

☐ *Payment enclosed. Kindly include $.50 postage and handling on order
up to $5.00. Above that, include 10% of total up to $20. Then 7% of
total. Thank you.*